Porter Profiles

Jaguar XK 120
The story of chassis 660725

Porter Press International

©Porter Press International

All rights reserved. No part of this publication may be reproduced, stored in a retrieval system or transmitted, in any form or by any means, electronic, mechanical, photocopying, recording or otherwise, without prior permission in writing from the publisher.

First published in November 2020

978-1-907085-80-2

Published by
Porter Press International Ltd

Hilltop Farm, Knighton-on-Teme, Tenbury Wells, WR15 8LY, UK
Tel: +44 (0)1584 781588
sales@porterpress.co.uk
www.porterpress.co.uk

Edited by James Page
Design & Layout by Martin Port

Printed by Gomer Press Ltd

COPYRIGHT
We have made every effort to trace and acknowledge copyright holders and we apologise in advance for any unintentional omission. We would be pleased to insert the appropriate acknowledgement in any subsequent edition.

Porter Profiles

Jaguar XK 120
The story of chassis 660725

Simon Ham

Porter Press International

Also published by Porter Press International

The Jaguar Portfolio
Ultimate E-type – The Competition Cars
Jaguar E-type – The Definitive History (2nd edition)
Original Jaguar XK (3rd edition)
Jaguar Design – A Story of Style
Saving Jaguar
The Jaguar Portfolio
Jaguar XK 120 Supersonic by Ghia
The All-American Hero and Jaguar's Racing E-types
E-type Jaguar DIY Restoration & Maintenance
Jaguar XK DIY Restoration & Maintenance
JUE 477 – The remarkable history & restoration of the world's first production Land-Rover

Exceptional Cars Series
No. 1 – Iso Bizzarrini – The remarkable history of A3/C 0222
No. 2 – Jaguar XK 120 – The remarkable history of JWK 651
No. 3 – Ford GT40 MkII – The remarkable history of 1016
No. 4 – The First Three Shelby Cobras
No. 5 – Aston Martin Ulster – The remarkable history of CMC 614
No. 6 – Maserati 4CLT – The remarkable history of chassis 1600
No. 7 – Ferrari 250 LM – The remarkable history of 6313
No. 8 – Ferrari 250 GT SWB – The remarkable history of 2689
No. 9 – Ferrari 857S – The remarkable history of 0578M
No. 10 – Alfa Romeo T33/TT/3 – The remarkable history of 115.72.002

Great Cars Series
No. 1 – Jaguar Lightweight E-type – The autobiography of 4 WPD
No. 2 – Porsche 917 – The autobiography of 917-023
No. 3 – Jaguar D-type – The autobiography of XKD 504
No. 4 – Ferrari 250 GT SWB – The autobiography of 2119 GT
No. 5 – Maserati 250F – The autobiography of 2528
No. 6 – ERA – The autobiography of R4D
No. 7 – Ferrari 250 GTO – The autobiography of 4153 GT
No. 8 – Jaguar Lightweight E-type – The autobiography of 49 FXN
No. 9 – Jaguar C-type – The autobiography of XKC 051
No. 10 – Lotus 18 – The autobiography of Stirling Moss's '912'
No. 11 – Ford GT40 – The autobiography of 1075
No. 12 – Alfa Romeo Monza – The autobiography of the celebrated 2211130
No. 13 – Bugatti Type 50 – The autobiography of Bugatti's first Le Mans car
No. 14 – Shelby Daytona Cobra – The autobiography of CSX2300

Porter Profiles Series
Austin-Healey 3000 – The story of DD 300
Jaguar D-type – The story of XKD 526

De Luxe leather-bound, signed, limited editions with slipcases are available for most titles.
Books available from retailers or signed copies direct from the publisher.
To order, simply phone +44 (0)1584 781588, visit the website or email sales@porterpress.co.uk

Keep up-to-date with news about current books and new releases at **www.porterpress.co.uk**

Contents

Introduction		6
1	Under fire in the Far East, 1951-1954	8
2	Scottish sojourn, 1954-1956	28
3	Conquering ice and snow, 1954-1959	36
4	In and out of hibernation, 1959-2004	44
5	Stopping power	54
6	Turbocharging an XK 120!	60
7	Postscript	68
8	Chassis 660725 in detail	70
Index		94

Introduction

If one were to enquire which car most people consider to be Jaguar's most famous, the likelihood is that they would say the E-type. Its timeless elegance, startling performance and sheer presence make it a natural choice. It is a car that transcends generations, justifiably held up as one of the great style icons of the 1960s. Yet paradoxically, and in the social and political context of its time, this is precisely why it could be argued that the introduction of the XK 120 in 1948 was an even more significant event than that of the E-type 13 years later.

While the 1960s heralded the return of – to coin a distinctly non-'60s phrase – the 'feel-good factor', the XK was born into the drab, predominantly nationalised, near-bankrupt fabric of post-war Britain, in which rationing would persist, in some cases, until 1954. The E-type was truly a car of its time, and although far more affordable – and arguably a better car – than its competitors, such as the Aston Martin DB4 and Ferrari 250 GT, the fact remains that alternatives to it did exist.

Conversely, at its launch at the 1948 Earls Court Motor Show, the XK 120 was simply other-worldly. Offering genuine 120mph performance, it was then officially the fastest production car in the world and was powered by a new 3.4-litre twin-cam engine, the likes of which had hitherto only been seen in pre-war greats such as the Alfa Romeo 8C and Bugatti Type 51. Although the new Sunbeam-Talbot, a very good car, and the Morris Minor, an utterly brilliant one, made their débuts on the same stage, nothing else at the show came close to offering the excitement, the hope, that the XK did.

During the XK 120's six-year lifespan, more than 12,000 were built – of which almost nine out of every 10 were supplied in left-hand-drive form. The mantra of the government at the time – 'Export or die' – accounts for much of this weighting; the commercial genius of Jaguar founder Sir William Lyons in identifying the US as his company's pre-eminent market is surely responsible for the remainder.

Although it was the Roadster version that had stolen the show at Earls Court, elegant Fixed Head and Drophead Coupé versions later became available, too. However, it was the Roadster that was by far the most numerous – indeed, more than half of the entire XK 120 production run were left-hand-drive Roadsters.

The car was an immediate success on track, its competition début in the *Daily Express*-sponsored one-hour sports car race at Silverstone in August 1949 culminating in an excellent one-two for Leslie Johnson and Peter Walker. The following year, Johnson's remarkable fifth place on the Mille Miglia, the heartbreaking retirement at Le Mans of the third-placed Johnson/Bert Hadley car after 21 hours, and Stirling Moss's maiden Tourist Trophy win were all highlights. The XK 120 also excelled in rallying, with Ian Appleyard – navigated by wife Pat, Sir William Lyons's daughter – taking a deserved win on the Alpine Rally, a feat they would repeat the following year.

As the adage goes, success breeds success, and Jaguar soon found that demand was outstripping supply. The XK 120 had been a huge hit in the US, particularly on the West Coast, and it soon became the vehicle of choice for many Hollywood stars. While Clark Gable was perhaps its greatest celebrity supporter – he is known to have owned at least four – other famous owners included Humphrey Bogart, Lauren Bacall, Tyrone Power and Robert Mitchum.

In 1954 – by which time it had spawned the magnificent C- and D-types, not to mention two of the XK engine's five Le Mans wins – the XK 120 was replaced with the XK 140. Less subtle in appearance but more refined than its predecessor, the later car was never quite taken to heart in the way the XK 120 was – many would maintain quite unfairly. Equipped with a very welcome rack-and-pinion steering system in place of the XK 120's worm-and-peg equivalent, the XK 140 gained another 30bhp from the XK engine and would remain in production until replaced by the XK 150 in 1957. In October 1960, by which time it started to show visible signs of age, the final XK 150 rolled off the production line at Jaguar's Browns Lane factory, to be replaced five months later with the E-type.

While it would be fatuous to suggest that without the XK there would have been no E-type, the latter certainly owes the former a great deal – not least the 3.8-litre straight-port cylinder head version of the XK engine that had, in fact, been introduced on the XK 150 S as long ago as 1958.

In broader terms, the legacy of the XK series is manifold. Immediate success opened Jaguar's eyes – even back in 1949 – to the public-relations benefits of racing and rallying, which ultimately led to its decision to pursue victory at Le Mans in the 1950s with such distinction. Furthermore, the rapturous reception that the XK 120 had received in America would set the tone for excellent relations between Coventry and the US for the next 25 or so years, with the E-type – or rather, XK-E – proving just as much of a hit across the Atlantic as its forebear.

Finally, in mechanical terms there can be few other engines with either the production lifespan or the versatility of the remarkable XK unit. Starting with the XK 120 in 1948 and finishing in 4.2-litre guise in the Daimler DS420 limousine in 1992, that it featured in the interim in Le Mans winners, family saloons, armoured vehicles and even fire engines is, perhaps, its greatest legacy of all.

Simon Ham

'Apart from now being the longest-serving XK 120 owner, I also consider myself the most fortunate, lucky, accidental, blessed, providential – call it what you will – owner. Why? Because no fictional script writer could have come up with the number or variety of experiences, both dangerous and funny, in so many different countries and environments, that any combination of car and man would experience together.'
Bob Henderson, January 2013

Chapter One
Under fire in the Far East 1951-1954

Few, if any, XK 120s can have enjoyed a more fascinating and varied life than chassis number 660725. Just under two-thirds of the total production was allocated to the Roadster (or, in official Jaguar terminology, Open Touring Sports), which had caused such a stir at the 1948 London Motor Show. Of that, 660725 was one of just 1,173 right-hand-drive Roadsters that were constructed.

The car had originally been ordered by Chan Lye Choon, a wealthy Singaporean businessman who later went on to win the 1958 Macau Grand Prix in an Aston Martin DB3S and the 1961 Johore Grand Prix in a Lola Mk1. Possessing the wherewithal to do so, if not the necessary contacts to be certain of securing one, Chan ordered two export-specification XK 120s from Jaguar in the hope that one might materialise. To his surprise, communication was received that both orders had been processed and that two cars were on their way to Singapore by boat.

Bob Henderson ventured out to Singapore in early 1950 on the P&O cargo ship *Shillong* as an 18-year-old trainee rubber trader working for the London-based firm of Hecht, Levis and Kahn. He spent a few weeks in the city before transferring offices to Kuala Lumpur, in what was then Malaya. There, operations were fronted by Hecht's subsidiary company, Anglo French and Bendixen, and as well as those in the capital there were further branch offices in Penang, Port Swettenham (now Port Klang) and Malacca. Despite being issued with a company Morris Minor – and never having owned a car before – Bob soon ditched this in favour of an MG TC with which he sped between the capital and Port Swettenham.

After having enjoyed a reception aboard a ship docked

A justifiably proud-looking Bob Henderson, together with his newly imported XK 120, in a typically Malay setting some time in 1951. The car already sports the local Perak Province registration number that it would retain throughout its time in the Far East.
Bob Henderson Collection

Under fire in the Far East • 1951-1954

Under fire in the Far East • 1951-1954

in Port Swettenham one evening, Bob and his then girlfriend – a former Miss Malaya contestant by the name of Connie MacGregor – were returning to Kuala Lumpur in the MG.

Bob takes up the story: 'We were "cruising" flat-out at well over 70mph when some headlights appeared behind us, caught up and passed us as though we were standing still! Impossible! The ignominy of it – the total puncturing of my youthful, arrogant ego…'

Suitably deflated, Bob arrived at his office the next morning and recounted the tale to his chief clerk, Thor Hor Chooi, who, from the description, surmised that the car in question must have been one of the new Jaguar XK 120s. From this point on – and, by his own admission, having never so much as heard of the marque – Bob simply had to get hold of one.

After some preliminary enquiries, it emerged that demand for the XK 120 was high and that it could be up to a year before one might be available through the Singaporean Jaguar dealership Cycle & Carriage (1926) Limited. Furthermore, Cycle & Carriage had a poor reputation for customer service, and rumours abounded that it was inflating prices by up to 20 percent to take advantage of the considerable local demand.

While not an especially spiritual or superstitious person, Bob is quick to acknowledge the part that good fortune has played in his life – and so it would prove when Chooi drew his attention to an advertisement in the back of *The Straits Times* only a week or so later. It had been placed by Chan Lye Choon, and advertised one of his XK 120s for sale. Both cars had been delivered with silver coachwork; one with red leather upholstery and one with blue. In common with his charming demeanour and good manners, which Bob was to appreciate when he met him, Chan made both cars available and would himself keep whichever car was not chosen by the prospective purchaser. In the end, Bob would opt for the car with the blue interior.

As a result of his ownership of the MG, Bob had made the acquaintance of two friendly local mechanics, Ah Hoi and Ah Kwan, who worked at Wearne Bros, the local Morris and MG dealership located on Pudu Road in Kuala Lumpur. In May 1951, all three somehow managed to squeeze into the MG, travelling down to Singapore to collect the XK. On arrival at the docks, they met Chan Lye Choon, who

Bob's then-girlfriend, former Miss Malaya contestant Connie MacGregor, pictured at the wheel of 660725 in Penang in late 1951.
Bob Henderson Collection

'We were "cruising" flat-out at well over 70mph when some headlights appeared behind us, caught up and passed us as though we were standing still! Impossible!'

The engine bay of 660725, clearly showing the rare early-type studless cylinder head of the timeless Jaguar XK engine. From November 1951 onwards, XK engines were fitted with three additional studs on the front of each cam cover to remedy the oil leaks that blighted earlier cars.
Bob Henderson Collection

An unusual low-level shot of 660725. The local registration number of AA 1771 was carefully chosen by its original purchaser, successful Singaporean racing driver and businessman Chan Lye Choon, because in Chinese culture letters and numbers with straight components are thought to bring good luck and prosperity.
Bob Henderson Collection

had already registered the car in Ipoh (in the Malay province of Perak) with the local registration AA 1771. Subsequently, it was established that in Chinese culture 'straight' numbers are considered more fortuitous than those with curves, and Chan had also thoughtfully affixed a silver St Christopher charm to the dashboard for good luck.

The car itself was a rare right-hand-drive export model, with the optional low-compression (7:1) engine to allow for potentially lower-grade fuels than might have been available in either the UK or US markets. Interestingly, being a relatively early car, the engine was still fitted with the so-called 'studless' cam covers, which were phased out on later cars due to their tendency to leak oil from the area immediately forward of the camshaft timing gear. Its destination meant that the XK was fitted with neither heater nor demister, although Bob would later be grateful for the recently introduced vertical side fresh-air vents, which would at least offer a modicum of circulation – the term 'cooling' somehow seems inappropriate given the equatorial climate – in the footwell area.

With the mechanics in the MG and Bob in the XK, they left Singapore for the journey back to Kuala Lumpur, although this was actually located in the state of Selangor and not in Perak where Chan had registered the car! In spite of it still being fitted with a restrictor bracket that limited the car to 2,500rpm – and hence around 60mph – the drive was a joy.

'Needless to say, the couple-of-hundred-mile drive back to Kuala Lumpur was a dream come true,' remembered Bob. 'The power, handling and ride were, to me, an absolute revelation and so exciting.'

Ah Hoi and Ah Kwan would continue to dote on the car throughout its time in Malaya, although Bob did, somewhat begrudgingly, use the Kuala Lumpur branch of Cycle & Carriage in order to have the throttle restrictor removed and its first service carried out once running-in duties had been completed. In effect, this was compulsory because removal of the bracket – which was sealed by the factory – by any other means led to the warranty of the car being invalidated.

Through his involvement in a project supplying generators to rural villages in Malaya, Bob became aware of a company in Hong Kong by the name of South China Iron Works. It made Mercedes diesel engines under licence that were used to power the generators, and boasted sufficient engineering talent to enable virtually everything to be produced in-house. In particular, Bob dealt with two brilliant engineers by the names of Dr Wu and Dr Su, both of whom took a particular interest in the XK. Without prompting, they took it upon themselves to design a pair of bespoke camshafts for it that were machined out of billet steel with an improved profile.

Bob noticed an immediate improvement in terms of both performance and throttle response, not to mention a rather more 'racy' exhaust note, although in due course he would also come to make a more interesting observation…

'Later on, Browns Lane "borrowed" these camshafts and I thought no more about it until, some years later, I was "miking" up some D-type camshafts that seemed remarkably similar. While I would not dream of making any obvious comments, I would suggest that historically many people were hanged on less circumstantial evidence!'

While it would be extremely difficult to prove, particularly with the passage of over 60 years, it is quite something to consider that the remarkable performance and flexibility of Jaguar's most iconic racing car may have owed something to two Hong Kong-based academics schooled in the design and development of diesel engines!

Taking advantage of the XK's sporting credentials – especially after the involvement of the good doctors – Bob took part in many competitive events in the area, which were of varying levels of organisation. While events such as the Kuala Lumpur Lornie Mile Speed Trial were organised by the Automobile Association of Malaya and were well established, others tended to be far more low-key. It was commonplace for rallies to be organised on the private roads of rubber plantations and estates, while driving tests took place on airfields such as Port Swettenham and even sand races were organised in locations such as Morib Beach, roughly 50 miles south-west of Kuala Lumpur.

Bob recalls that, 'Many events were spontaneous, emanating from a bar or club conversation – or bet – on a Friday or Saturday night for the following Sunday, and were largely unreported or even recorded, apart from who bought the next round of beers or Singapore Slings!'

Occasionally, there would also be good-natured (but high-speed) 'races' with fellow road users, one regular adversary being a 1,000cc Vincent motorbike ridden by young man dressed only in shorts, a singlet, flip-flops and without any form of head or eye protection! One of the most potent motorcycles of the time, the Vincent and Bob would regularly duel at speeds in excess of 100mph, with the Vincent's rider merely tilting his head to one side – and as close to the fuel tank as possible – to minimise both wind resistance

> 'Many events were spontaneous, emanating from a bar or club conversation – or bet – on a Friday or Saturday night, and were largely unreported or even recorded, apart from who bought the next round of beers or Singapore Slings!'

A cheery-looking Bob preparing to compete at the Port Swettenham Driving Tests in 1951. Located 25 miles to the east of Kuala Lumpur, the airfield had been an Allied aircraft service base during World War Two and gave rise to a strong local 'ex-pat' motoring community. Post-independence, the town was renamed Port Kelang in 1972.
Bob Henderson Collection

Under fire in the Far East • 1951-1954

Bob Henderson competing in 660725 at the Lornie Mile, a one-mile sprint organised in Kuala Lumpur by the Automobile Association of Malaya. The protection for the drivers from the water hazard on the left and for the spectators on the right from the passing cars appears to have been equally cursory.
Bob Henderson Collection

and the ingress of all manner of tropical insects into the eyes.

'I never actually met him or knew his name. We were just two lads with our toys enjoying the odd chance to try them out in company. So – sadly, in retrospect – we only exchanged a wave and the odd salute in mutual respect.'

Since 1948, a state of emergency had existed in Malaya, the communist Malayan National Liberation Army (MNLA) in effect having declared war against the incumbent British rule, with the aim of establishing an independent, communist Malaya. Pockets of Communist Terrorist (CT) activity existed throughout rural areas, with the area around Bentong in Pahang – roughly 50 miles north-east of Kuala Lumpur – being a particular hotbed. Indeed, in the same province, Fraser's Hill had in 1951 been the site of the assassination of Sir Henry Gurney, then High Commissioner for Malaya.

Given the volatility of the situation, it was only a matter of time before counter-insurgency units – consisting of both military and civilian personnel – established themselves in an attempt to neutralise the CT threat. Although disbanded following the formal signing of the Japanese surrender in September 1945, several members of the SOE-organised Force 136 had stayed on in the area; some had found gainful employment in areas such as mining and the plantation business. Bob's counterpart at Anglo French and Bendixen's Malacca office, Alan Acton, was himself a former Force 136 agent.

At about this time, an ostensibly innocent organisation, the Hash House Harriers, became a popular social outlet for many British ex-pats in the vicinity of Kuala Lumpur. It had been formed in 1938 to promote both exercise and social drinking, but the Kuala Lumpur Ampang chapter – of which Bob would be a founding member – would prove a useful front for the type of covert anti-CT activities described above.

Having been a keen Army Cadet, promising athlete, crack shot and a capable navigator at school, Bob, although young, was well qualified in his role as a 'Hashie'. Thanks to the mentoring that was received from several of the former Force 136 agents – with their exhaustive knowledge of jungle-based warfare in the area – the Ampang chapter soon became a formidable foil to the CTs, although Bob is keen to dispel any notion that this could

Hash House Harriers

A multi-faceted and multi-national confederation that flourishes to this day, the Hash House Harriers remains a recreational running organisation with the apparently contradictory aims of promoting exercise and social drinking in roughly equal measure. Founded in Selangor in 1938 by a group of British expatriates and military officers – several of whom lived in an annex of the Selangor Club colloquially known as the Hash House – activities centred around a select band of runners (the hares) setting off in advance and laying a trail that the remainder of the assembled group (variously known as the harriers, hounds or pack) would attempt to follow. It was frequently described as 'a drinking club with a running problem', and the successful conclusion of each run would be toasted with beer and, in the distant past, cigarettes.

The inscription on club membership cards during the 1950s identified four major aims of the organisation: to promote physical fitness among members; to get rid of weekend hangovers; to acquire a good thirst and satisfy it in beer; to persuade the older members that they are not as old as they feel.

Having experienced considerable growth in and around Kuala Lumpur in the 1950s, a Singapore chapter of the organisation was established in 1962 that was a precursor to rapid 1970s expansion in areas including Europe, North America, the South Pacific and even Antarctica. Recent estimates suggest that there could be as many as 100,000 active members distributed across the 184 countries known to currently host one or more chapters.

Members of the Royal Selangor Club in Kuala Lumpur (left) are said to have formed the Hash House Harriers in 1938 in a bid to help rid themselves of weekend hangovers as well as promote fitness among their group.
Alamy

However, in the context of the prevailing situation in 1950s Malaya, the group – and in particular the Kuala Lumpur-based Ampang chapter of which Bob was a member – had an altogether more sinister motive.

'The Hash House Harriers as an organisation was basically innocent,' remembers Bob, 'but our Ampang chapter was not, and the HHH banner was just used by us as a very convenient smokescreen. This was to fool the Min Yuen communist spies and reduce any other gossip that might lead to security problems. You might say that in some ways the Ampang chapter was a sort of unofficial resurrection of the original Force 136.

'The "Ampangites" were a unique bunch in as much as they were largely comprised of disaffected civilians who quite successfully – while acting covertly in their spare time along with Special Branch's connivance – took the war to the CTs in their jungle lairs. A sort of civilian "Ferret" force, based on the military examples of Major-General Wingate's Burma Chindits and Lieutenant-Colonel Walker's Malayan Ferret Force.'

Under fire in the Far East • 1951-1954

Connie and 660725, outside Bob's Company 'Mess' in Kuala Lumpur, some time in late 1951.
Bob Henderson Collection

have been for the purposes of financial gain.

'No doubt some of our modern-day bleating liberals will try to claim that the Hashie "Ampangers" were either vigilantes or mercenaries – or even both. Nothing could be further from the truth. Despite the high financial rewards offered for any CT captures or kills, not a single penny was ever accepted by any Hashie, despite quite a lot of pressure often being put on some of them to accept a reward for their, in effect, public service.'

In view of the need for Bob to frequently move around between the branch offices of Kuala Lumpur, Port Swettenham and Klang, he was more than relieved when the trusty works Morris Minor had been replaced by his MG TC – and once again when the TC was superseded by the Jaguar.

'The XK 120 enabled me to reduce the time I was a potential target for CT guns,' he remembers, 'particularly at night, which was more dangerous because there were fewer military patrols about and the CTs could see a car's headlights well in advance of their arrival. This would give them more time to set an ambush or to fell a tree across the road. As such, the Jaguar's speed was a life-saving bonus.'

On one memorable occasion, Bob's friend Basil (regrettably his surname remains unknown) of the Army Kinema Corporation – a government organisation that operated no fewer than 29 mobile cinemas in Malaya at the time – had broken down in his AKC van near Bentong. Bob received a message requesting assistance, and duly set off in the XK 120. After several miles, and having just passed a travelling platoon of Malay regiment troops, Bob felt an intense pain in his right elbow. After a moment or two, he deduced that he – and, infuriatingly, the XK – had been hit by a CT sniper's bullet. He immediately stopped the car and reversed back to the ambush point. By this time, the platoon had arrived and were already firing at the sniper, who was attempting to make his escape through the dense jungle.

Bob set off on foot, determined to exact revenge with the .38 revolver he carried at all times. Although gaining on the CT, he heard two bullets whistle past his head, and the CT fell to the ground. Bob initially feared that these had been aimed at him by another terrorist, although various Malay shouts quickly confirmed that

The Malayan Emergency

Inspector Tun Hamzah of the Malayan Police Special Branch conducting a briefing during the Malayan Emergency. Both Prime Minister Churchill and Malayan High Commissioner Sir Gerald Templer credited the MPSB as having been pivotal in infiltrating the Communist-led Malayan National Liberation Army and in stifling the insurgent threat.
Alamy

Sparked by the murder of three European rubber plantation managers in the northern state of Perak in June 1948, the British declared a State of Emergency in Malaya that was to endure for the next 12 years. The Malayan National Liberation Army (MNLA) – the quasi-military wing of the Malayan Communist Party (MCP) – sought to overthrow British rule, and to establish an independent Malaya. Led by the notorious Chin Peng and supported by the majority of the Chinese Malay population, the MNLA was intent on destroying government and military property, destabilising Malaya's rubber industry and spreading communist doctrine.

The initial British response was to mobilise six Gurkha, three British and two Malay battalions, with National Servicemen being sent as reinforcements from August 1948 onwards. In response to the heightened threat – and at the behest of director of operations Lieutenant-General Sir Harold Briggs – the British introduced a wide range of counter-terrorism measures, including obtaining intelligence to identify areas of Communist Terrorist (CT) activity, increasing security in those areas most at risk and mobilising volunteer auxiliary forces such as the Malayan Home Guard. The latter operated a series of checkpoints aimed at cutting off the flow of supplies to the jungle-based CTs.

In an attempt to separate the CTs from their passive supporters, a controversial programme of resettling the Chinese Malays into purpose-built villages followed. Some 400,000 had been rehoused by the end of 1951, most of whom had been lured by the provision of good-quality housing, clean water, education and medical care. This programme suffered a setback in October 1951 when the High Commissioner for Malaya, Sir Henry Gurney, was assassinated.

In January 1952, General Sir Gerald Templer succeeded Gurney as High Commissioner, an appointment widely viewed as heralding the end of the conflict. His conciliatory approach, which focused on the need to win the 'hearts and minds' of the population, resonated with the Chinese Malays, as did his promise to grant Malaya independence in the event of a guerrilla surrender.

Malaya became an independent federation in August 1957, with the British-backed Tunku Abdul Rahman as Prime Minister, and by 1958 the last pockets of guerrilla resistance had surrendered at Telok Anson in Perak.

However, the State of Emergency was not officially declared over until 31 July 1960, by which time 6,700 guerrilla fighters, 1,800 Malayan and Commonwealth troops, and some 3,000 civilians had lost their lives.

they had in fact emanated from the platoon.

'He dropped like a stone as I reached him. I could see he had one bullet in the head and another in the shoulder. I simply put two more into him for good luck and felt a lot better for it. How dare they even think of shooting my precious XK!'

A brief assessment of Bob's wounds afterwards confirmed that he had, in fact, been shot twice. There was a considerable amount of blood coming from a sizeable wound along his right forearm, while a second bullet had taken a small chunk of flesh from his right hip, although luckily both slugs had missed bones and vital organs.

The Malay troops offered welcome medical assistance and insisted that he get to a hospital as soon as possible. With his customary loyalty and sense of duty, Bob did this only after first rescuing Basil!

The XK was also looking slightly the worse for wear, its aluminium door skin having been punctured by the two bullets. After brief enquiries, some panel-beater associates of Ah Hoi and Ah Kwan soon remedied the situation by reskinning the door at their premises – ironically, just behind the Jaguar agent on Batu Road in Kuala Lumpur.

The original silver paintwork had started to fade after continual exposure to the tropical sun, so it was decided that the car should be treated to a respray at the same time. A fetching shade of dark blue was decided upon, which complemented the lighter blue trim.

Throughout their time in Malaya, Bob and his trusty XK were involved in many anti-CT ambushes. With much of the

After prolonged exposure to the tropical sun, and with the driver's side door skin having been perforated by several Communist bullets, 660725 was treated to a respray in a suitably distinguished shade of dark blue. The car is seen here prior to the rear lights, windscreen surround, spats and hubcaps being refitted.
Bob Henderson Collection

> 'The usual procedure under fire was to run the gauntlet, but if the way was blocked then the preferred option was to drive off the road into the rough'

Throughout Bob's time in Malaya, the XK was tended to by his loyal and trusted mechanics Ah Hoi and Ah Kwan. Both officially worked for Wearne Bros, the BMC dealership in Kuala Lumpur, but lavished attention on the car in their spare time. Here, they pose with Bob shortly after the respray, with the rear lights and bumpers yet to be refitted. It would appear that the rear brakes are being worked upon at the same time.
Bob Henderson Collection

Under fire in the Far East • 1951-1954

area around Kuala Lumpur being of basically similar geography, and many of the roads being of similar size and construction, Bob even adopted a (broadly) standardised response in the event of a terrorist threat ahead.

'The usual procedure under fire was just to run the gauntlet, but if the way was blocked then the preferred option was to drive off the road into the rough or ditch on the side away from the firing, which meant that the car – even if it was on its side – gave some cover from the flying bullets and gave a barricade to return fire from safety.'

With Bob increasingly committed to combatting the CT threat in his spare time, the effect of spending so much time in the jungle began to take its toll on him. He was feeling generally unwell for long periods, so his bosses in Singapore eventually decided that he should return home to the UK for a few months to recuperate. The sickness itself would never be diagnosed – although there were certain symptoms in common with malaria – and rest was deemed the best course of action. Prior to returning home, Bob entrusted his beloved XK to Freddie Pope – sometime Singapore Motor Club President and 1953 Johore Grand Prix winner in his own XK 120 – for storage at his garage near the docks in Singapore.

It was during this supposed spell of recuperation that Bob would have another close shave in an XK – albeit this time from the passenger seat. He had been introduced to Tony van Beugen Bik, the son of a Dutch business associate of his father's, who also had an XK 120. They decided to travel up to Charterhall race track in the Scottish Borders, but just passing Catterick Garrison Tony lost control of the car in spectacular fashion and crashed into a stone cottage. During the impact, Bob was thrown out and suffered serious facial and dental injuries, although on reflection considered himself fortunate not to have been decapitated by the XK's windscreen.

Two spells in hospital – one in nearby Darlington and one in Guy's in central London – one bout of septicaemia, and several plastic-surgery operations later, Bob headed back east once again, this time to Jakarta, in Indonesia. He'd joined a new firm, although the work would be along much the same lines as he had done previously, with a strong emphasis on trading rubber and tea.

During his time at home, Bob had noticed that an aftermarket hardtop for the XK 120 was now

Two additional photographs of 660725 following its respray, taken in the garden at the home of Bob's friend Basil (his surname regrettably is not known) in Kuala Lumpur. The rather unsightly four exposed bolts on the lower front valance are the mountings onto which the XKs elegant 'bumperettes' would be refitted.
Bob Henderson Collection

being produced by a company called Universal Laminations in Bayswater, West London. These were finished in leatherette and featured novel sliding sidescreens, so Bob ordered one because he thought it advisable given the likely monsoons he would have to contend with in Indonesia. It was sent directly to Southampton docks and to the ship that he was due to take to Singapore before heading onward to Jakarta. In Singapore, the hardtop was delivered to Freddie Pope for fitment. At the same time, Bob's .38 revolver was secreted in the XK's sump and several boxes of ammunition squirrelled away in the headlight nascelles! Given the inherently unstable nature of the area at the time – and following his Bentong experience – Bob would not be taking any chances again…

After a brief stop in Singapore, he travelled onto Jakarta, with the XK following a fortnight or so later. Rumour had it that there was only one other XK 120 in the whole of Indonesia at the time, due to the punitive import taxes payable and relative lack of local wealth. Fortunately, Bob was permitted to import his XK tax-free, although the Hillman Minx that he was issued with as a company car had reputedly cost more locally than the company

Under fire in the Far East • 1951-1954

A rare image taken from above, showing off the XK's timeless lines and the fierce tropical sun to equal effect. The presence of front indicators and the small enamel Union Jack emblem to the rear of the front wheel suggest that the photograph was taken during the car's time in Jakarta, Indonesia.
Bob Henderson Collection

Another photograph of 660725's engine bay, clearly showing the etched brass chassis plate to the right of the rear exhaust manifold. As well as the chassis number itself, the plate contained other information including engine, body and gearbox numbers, as well as recommended lubricants and valve clearances.
Bob Henderson Collection

chairman's Rolls-Royce had back in London!

The XK 120 was relatively under-utilised in Indonesia, largely due to the tiresome Jakarta traffic and also to having use of a company car. Throughout its time in Java, it was serviced by the local Hillman agents who, among other things, fitted flashing Scintilla indicators that were considered very advanced at the time. As expected, the hardtop was a godsend during the rain season, although the rather apologetic single-speed windscreen wipers meant that forward visibility did not always match the level of comfort of those inside.

Following a three-month spell in the wild jungles of Borneo assessing the communist threat there – during which time the XK remained in Jakarta – Bob once again started to suffer from the mysterious jungle fever. After much deliberation and soul-searching, he decided to return home to the United Kingdom once again. The XK was booked onto a ship to Southampton from the main port at Tanjung Priok, and left a couple of days after Bob flew home on a KLM-operated Lockheed Super Constellation. It would be six weeks before the two were reunited once again.

'The XK was booked onto a ship to Southampton from the main port at Tanjung Priok, and left a couple of days after Bob flew home on a KLM-operated Lockheed Super Constellation'

During Bob's period of enforced recuperation back in the UK in 1952, 660725 was transported by train from Kuala Lumpur to Singapore, for storage at the garage of renowned Far Eastern XK racer Freddie Pope. It is pictured here being loaded up.
Bob Henderson Collection

Under fire in the Far East • 1951-1954

Chapter Two
Scottish sojourn 1954-1956

After returning to the UK for a second spell of sick leave in 1954, Bob's life was to ultimately to take a drastically different course, and would not involve a return to the Far East, as had originally been planned. He had been corresponding with a young pen-pal, Prue Lapworth, for some time but little did he – or anyone else – know that this would lead to him marrying her on Valentine's Day of the following year.

There had also been a long-running period of legal correspondence between Bob and the insurance company dealing with Tony van Beugen Bik's accident at Catterick, and this too would, indirectly, have a profound effect on the course of his life. Bob's solicitor had mentioned that he had a client by the name of Robert (Bob) Short, who was looking for a personal assistant with sound mechanical knowledge to assist at his company, Short Aviation. Short was distantly related to Oswald and Eustace Short, who in 1897 had founded Short Brothers, the company that would produce the Short Stirling heavy bomber and Short Sunderland flying boat patrol bombers that had been used to great effect in World War Two.

Short Aviation had purchased about 70 ex-Navy de Havilland Mosquitoes from the Ministry of Defence, the majority of which were based at the Fleet Air Arm station at Lossiemouth on the Moray Firth in Scotland. The company had obtained a contract to supply 20 aircraft to the Israeli Air Force, which continued to use them for both photo-reconnaissance and combat purposes up until the end of the Suez Crisis in 1956.

Initially, Bob would be based at Short's offices at Whyteleafe in Surrey, although he would soon transfer to RNAS (Royal Naval Air Station) Culham in Oxfordshire

A poignant and charming portrait of Bob's first wife, Prue, together with the newly re-registered MOW 523, near their new home in Lossiemouth, Scotland around February 1955. Prue's hand is partially obscuring the non-standard 'Leaping Cat' bonnet mascot that the car had acquired by then. Tragically, she succumbed to a rare form of stomach cancer in 1978, aged just 43.
Bob Henderson Collection

Scottish sojourn • 1954-1956

Scottish sojourn • 1954-1956

to familiarise himself with the mechanics of Short's half-dozen or so Mosquitoes that resided there. He was also educated on procedural matters, such as inspection schedules and component certification, which would prove invaluable in the ensuing years.

Shortly afterwards, Bob transferred to Lossiemouth and within a month found himself in the position of chief engineer and junior test pilot. He rented a flat in Lossiemouth itself and – perhaps more importantly – managed to find a lock-up garage around the corner in which to house the XK 120, newly arrived from Singapore and now bearing the UK registration MOW 523.

Within a month of its arrival, Bob caught a train down south to pick up the Jaguar, returning almost immediately with the car packed full of Mosquito spares and, in particular, numerous boxes of valuable platinum-tipped spark plugs.

MOW was immediately pressed into action in Scotland, regardless of the weather. At the time, Short Aviation frequently enlisted the help of experienced Mosquito pilot Peter Nock to deliver aircraft to the IAF once their recommissioning had been completed. Indeed, by the start of 1955, Peter had delivered 10 Mosquitoes to Israel and – being based west of London – relied upon Bob for frequent pick-ups from Inverness railway station.

In his memoirs, Peter was moved to comment that: 'Getting to Lossiemouth meant the night train to Inverness, from where Bob Henderson always collected me in his Jaguar XK 120. On one occasion, the roads were solid snow and we still made the journey in not much over the hour. Luckily, I happened to have my parachute bag on my lap, and it was very comforting to have this between me and the windscreen!'

From time to time, the trusty XK would get pressed into service on the airfield as well. Short Aviation did not have an aircraft tow vehicle of its own, so it was reliant on its 'landlord' – the Navy, because the base was still technically HMS Fulmar at that time – to loan it the use of one when required. On more than one occasion, Bob would grow tired of waiting for one to appear, so a cable would be attached from the Mosquito tailwheel to the Jaguar's rear dumb irons, and the roughly six-ton aircraft towed carefully behind it with remarkably little fuss. However, Bob did observe that one had to account for the considerable inertia of the aircraft and slow

> 'Within a month of its arrival, Bob caught a train down south to pick up the Jaguar, returning with the car packed full of Mosquito spares'

An uncharacteristically hirsute Bob leaning on the Jaguar's rear wing in Lossiemouth, some time in early 1956. The Mosquito behind appears in the colours of the Israeli Air Force; it was one of 20 such examples supplied by Bob's erstwhile employer, Short Aviation.
Bob Henderson Collection

MOW 523 photographed outside Bob's family home at Court Echo in Surrey. The omission of the XK's distinctive radiator grille suggests that the car was receiving some form of remedial attention or modification from its devoted owner at the time.
Bob Henderson Collection

down progressively in order to avoid an almighty crunch!

On other occasions, and only when a blind eye was turned by the authorities, races would be staged at the airfield between MOW and the aircraft. Not surprisingly, the XK would get off to the superior start, although the two were generally neck and neck by around 90mph – the usual take-off speed for an unladen Mosquito. However, such races would be a little more one-sided against the TR33 aircraft-carrier variants because

The Wooden Wonder

If the Hawker Hurricane is justifiably lauded as the unsung hero of the Battle of Britain, arguably a similar accolade can be attributed to the de Havilland Mosquito for the remainder of the war. Although the Mosquito did not see active service until September 1941, it was instrumental in maintaining Britain's air superiority over the Luftwaffe and was, by general consensus, the world's first successful multi-role combat aircraft. Equally accomplished in fighter, fighter-bomber, photo-reconnaissance, trainer, courier or torpedo bomber roles, no fewer than 33 different variants of this remarkable aeroplane existed during the war. That a further seven followed in peacetime – by when the jet engine had already been identified as the way forward – merely underlines its capabilities.

Designed by Geoffrey de Havilland himself, the Mosquito remarkably went from drawing board to maiden flight in a little over 11 months. It made extensive use of wood in its structure, which had the multiple benefits of being in plentiful supply, easy to work with, of a good strength-to-weight ratio and, crucially, of a low radar signature. Furthermore, the relative lack of specialised equipment required meant that the production of the fuselage and wings could take place in repurposed furniture factories accustomed to batch production and rapid turnaround. It was entirely appropriate that the Mosquito soon acquired the affectionate nickname 'The Wooden Wonder'.

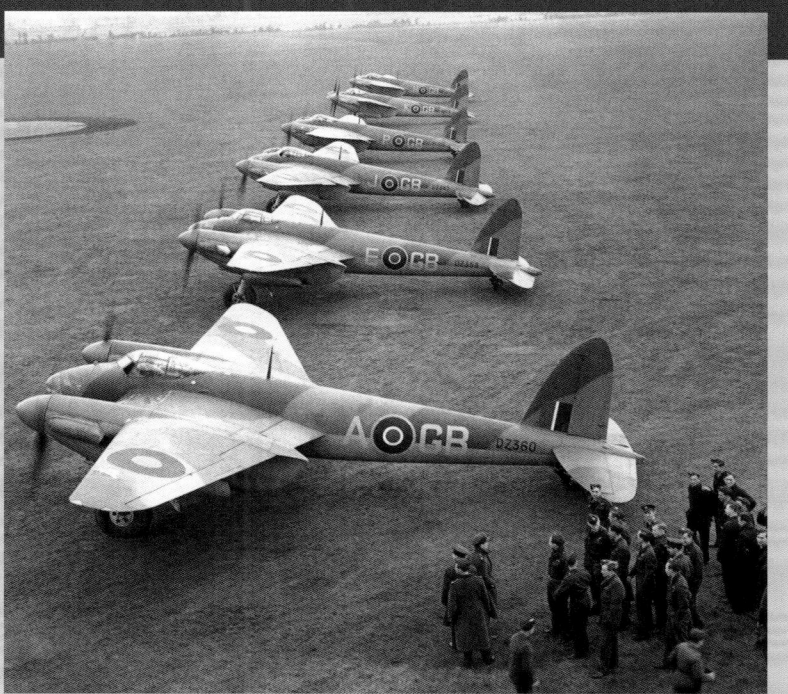

Mosquito Mk IVs of 105 Squadron RAF, pictured in 1942. The Mk IV entered active service in May of that year, and was instrumental in securing Allied air superiority in the second half of the war. Alamy

Powered by two Rolls-Royce Merlin V12 engines of up to 1,700hp each, the magic of the aircraft lay in its agility and versatility. The definitive light-bomber version, the Mk XVI, had a wingspan of only 54 feet and weighed just 6.3 tons empty, yet could carry a bomb payload of 4,000 pounds. In comparison, the Boeing B17 'Flying Fortress' – mainstay of the American bombing effort during World War Two – had a payload of only an additional 500 pounds, yet virtually double the wingspan and an empty weight of over 16 tons.

Although not an easy aeroplane to fly due to its high power-to-weight ratio and high wing loading, the Mosquito excelled in low-level 'hit and run' raids, famously blowing the walls of the prison in Amiens to liberate 250 or so French Resistance fighters, and devastating the Gestapo headquarters in Copenhagen. Indeed, eyewitness reports at the time reported that the latter attack was so low-level that aeroplanes literally flew down the boulevards of the Danish capital and banked into side streets.

Officially the aircraft was replaced by the English Electric Canberra in 1951, although it saw active service as late as 1956 during the Suez Crisis. Some 7,781 Mosquitoes were constructed in total, all but 1,071 during the war. However, due to the nature of its construction, degradation was high, and only 30 non-flying and four airworthy examples are known to survive – an inadequate reflection of the impact of this most remarkable of aircraft.

their four-bladed propellers (as opposed to the usual three) ensured better throttle response and usually led to the aeroplane forging ahead by the time they'd reached 80mph or so.

One of Bob's favourite stories involving MOW in Scotland concerns the time he took his (UK) driving test in the car, having hitherto relied upon its international counterpart. This took place in Elgin the night after a particularly heavy snowfall, and it was clear from the outset that the examiner was intent on going for a drive in such an exotic car, whether advisable to do so in the conditions or not. After less than five minutes, he informed Bob that he had passed the test and politely asked him to demonstrate exactly what the car could do.

'We set off into the unploughed and often single-track snowy roads in the hills behind Elgin,' Bob recalled. 'We ploughed through snow drifts, often bouncing along from opposite snow bank to snow bank, with quite a lot of opposite-lock steering, while powering through long corners at speeds that would not normally have been regarded as sane even on a clear, dry road.'

After the impromptu rally stage, and suitably sated, the examiner returned to the test centre and was heard to declare that all other driving tests were cancelled that day due to the adverse weather conditions!

Towards the end of 1955, it emerged that the Navy did not wish Short Aviation to remain at Lossiemouth, and with the Israeli contract all but completed, it was clear that changes were afoot. Short had been negotiating to move to an airfield in Banff, Aberdeenshire, but for reasons Bob was never made fully aware of, this did not materialise. Subsequently, Short offered him a job servicing civilian Miles Magister aircraft, but from Bob's perspective this was rather a backwards step and one that he opted not to pursue.

A chance conversation with Peter Nock, however, led to an introduction to a company in Ottawa by the name of Spartan Air Services. It had purchased some ex-RAF Mosquitoes and was looking for engineers who were experienced on the aircraft, and on Rolls-Royce Merlin engines in particular. Although Bob's employment there was not confirmed, he and the now-pregnant Prue opted to emigrate to Canada during the spring of 1956, and to embark on a new chapter in their (and MOW's) itinerant lives.

> 'We ploughed through snow drifts, often bouncing along from opposite snow bank to snow bank, with quite a lot of opposite-lock steering'

A dapper Bob, again at the family home at Court Echo, shortly after MOW's 1955 return from Indonesia.
Bob Henderson Collection

Scottish sojourn • 1954-1956

Chapter Three

Conquering ice and snow 1956-1959

Sailing from Liverpool to Montreal aboard the venerable Greek ship *Olympus*, both Bob and Prue endured a miserable few days crossing the Atlantic Ocean, especially poor Prue who, in addition to the lamentable sanitary conditions and dreadful food, had the rigours of morning sickness to contend with.

Having purchased some ex-RAF Mosquitoes that were in desperate need of some remedial attention, the management at Spartan Air Services viewed Bob as something of a 'guru', and his time was to be divided between carrying out work himself and passing on his considerable knowledge to other members of the company's keen (if mildly clueless) workforce.

In May 1956, MOW 523 arrived in Montreal, the car being transported onwards to Ottawa by rail. Given the pleasant late-spring climate, the weather equipment on the car (or lack thereof, because it was a tropical export model without either heater or demister) was not likely to be an immediate problem, but would require addressing before the onset of winter. Bob therefore set about sourcing an aftermarket item – an ingenious solution being found in a unit that secured to the windscreen with two 'sucker pads' and plugged into the cigarette lighter.

As in the Far East, Bob soon established that the local Jaguar dealer's attitude to aftersales service left much to be desired. There was a general unwillingness to assist any owners who had not purchased their cars locally, and even those who had done so frequently noted that their cars returned from service running less smoothly than they had done beforehand! Indeed, the situation soon deteriorated to the point that Bob took on servicing and repair work for

In Canada, and as part of his preparations for the 1956-'57 ice-racing season and the Canadian International Winter Rally, Bob would practice techniques such as powersliding and cadence braking in deserted snow-covered car parks, as seen here.
Bob Henderson Collection

Conquering ice and snow • 1956-1959

Conquering ice and snow • 1956-1959

If the venerable XK's side vents had been vital in keeping its occupants (relatively) cool in Malaya, the aftermarket demister unit sourced by Bob – clearly seen here at the base of the driver's side windscreen – was equally important during the car's time in Canada. Surely few XKs can boast of prolonged exposure to two more different climates.
Bob Henderson Collection

several other Jaguar owners and established a business – European Car Specialists – as a sideline to his work at SAS. That the main Jaguar importer and distributor in Montreal would refer unhappy Ottawan Jaguar owners to Bob, rather than to their local dealer, spoke volumes.

Having been in Ottawa a few months, both Bob and Prue – now proud parents of a baby son, Laird, who had been born in November 1956 – were gradually building up a circle of friends, and they became members of the local Ottawa Motor Club. Although the majority of their events tended to be rather pedestrian regularity and treasure hunt-style rallies, some of the more adventurous members would occasionally venture a few miles south-west of the city to the Britannia Bay area, where in winter ice racing would take place on the frozen Ottawa River.

Although the organisation of the Britannia Bay Ice Races was relatively low-key, they did operate a four-class structure, stratified by cubic capacity. Ever the lateral thinker, Bob reasoned that, while the XK was 3,442cc in total, this merely consisted of six cylinders of 574cc each, and so by the simple removal of one (or more) spark plug leads

> 'He got childishly frustrated when I beat him and his supposedly superior car in each heat, to such an extent that he kicked and smashed in the car's bodywork'

the capacity could be artificially altered to suit the various classes. As a result, the removal of one lead would ensure that the (now five-cylinder) car dropped into the up to 3-litre class, while the removal of three ensured that it could compete in the up to 2-litre category, thereby ensuring possibly the only recorded competitive outing for an XK 'triple'!

In contrast to the Britannia Bay event, the ice races organised at Sainte-Agathe-des-Monts, some 60 miles north-west of Montreal, were an altogether more serious proposition. Organised by the Laurentian Auto Club (LAC) on the Lac des Sables just outside the town of Sainte-Agathe itself, these frequently attracted entries from other Canadian provinces, as well as those from over the border in Vermont and upstate New York. The 1957 event attracted a good-quality entry, including wealthy construction company heir Stanley McRobert in his newly acquired Jaguar XKSS – chassis number XKD 575, aka XKSS 716.

Although McRobert also owned an alloy-bodied XK 120 – chassis 670004, only the fourth left-hand-drive car constructed – Bob had little time for him, remarking that he appeared spoilt and somewhat lacking in manners: 'He got childishly frustrated when I beat him and his supposedly superior car in each heat, to such an extent that he kicked and smashed in the car's bodywork behind the wheels because he claimed it was causing too much drag against the snow banks and slowing him down.'

McRobert and Bob went head-to-head in the final, with both exchanging places throughout the race. By his own admission, Bob let his dislike of his opponent get the better of him and owns up to 'baiting him a bit', so much so that a diminutive 750cc Renault 4CV slipped through at the final corner, demoting Bob to second place and a near-incandescent McRobert to third!

McRobert proceeded to then take out his frustrations on the poor XKSS once again, prior to protesting Bob for running studded tyres – an allegation swiftly and correctly dismissed by the organisers.

Within the admittedly relatively sedate and amateurish confines of the Ottawa Motor Club, Bob had acquired a reputation as a capable driver on snow and ice, and it was suggested to him that he should enter the forthcoming Canadian

Conquering ice and snow • 1956-1959

International Winter Rally. Organised by the quaintly named British Empire Motor Club, the rally started from Toronto and Montreal simultaneously (rather as the Monte Carlo Rally used to) and took in a route encompassing the area around the St Lawrence River near the US border, before heading up into Northern Ontario and the Laurentian Mountains in Quebec.

While MOW 523 would be generally well suited to the event, certain modifications were required to cope with the ferocious cold of the Canadian winter, during which temperatures could drop to as low as -40 degrees. For the first time, the car was fitted with a heater (sourced from a Land-Rover and mounted on top of the gearbox tunnel), while an ingenious adjustable radiator blind system was devised that permitted a swatch of thick carpet to be raised or lowered inside the XK's distinctive radiator grille to regulate cooling.

The boot of the car was filled with essential items such as fuel, oil, tools, rope and a hand winch, while a folding shovel and traction mats – made from bulletproof fuel-tank cladding, as used on Mosquitoes – were carried inside the car.

The event lasted for two full days and two nights and required two drivers, both of whom were to be in possession of a competition licence. Bob enlisted the help of Tim Plottier, a Frenchman married to an English friend of Prue's, although Bob's intention from the outset was to drive the event single-handed and use Tim only for the most rudimentary navigation and for what might be termed 'recovery liaison'. There was a widely held belief among competitors that, in Quebec, bystanders – and, specifically, farmers equipped with tow vehicles – were far more receptive to those requesting assistance in French than they were to those doing so in English!

Opting to start from Montreal, the rally started off eventfully for MOW 523, with a sticking throttle after a couple of hours resulting in an unscheduled encounter with a snow bank. However, judicious use of the traction mats and some light digging ensured that time loss was kept to a minimum. The first night passed largely without issue, although good fortune certainly played its part.

'The rest of the night became a blur,' said Bob, 'constantly sliding, bouncing off snow banks and riding other people's ruts cut into the packed snow, a bit like tram lines – and hoping that none of them led off the road! Riding the ruts was a new technique to me, but I warmed to it and found myself going faster and faster… I developed a new feeling of being "at one" with the car, full of confidence and optimism.'

As the next morning dawned, a combination of poor conditions and tiredness led to multiple cars having picked up time penalties, with Bob and Tim one of only three Montreal crews still with a clean sheet. Bob's recollection of the first full day of the rally is somewhat limited, save for the fact that it was a gloriously sunny one – and that they narrowly avoided a head-on crash with a police car! This he puts down to a combination of a momentary lapse in concentration, his becoming a little blasé as far as the conditions were concerned, and the fact that the police car in question was the first car of any kind that they'd encountered for more than an hour.

That night afforded a few hours of valuable rest and a shower at a lodge just outside Sunbury, Ontario, roughly 30 miles from the shores of Lake Huron, before the crews headed south to Toronto.

The final day started badly, with Tim making a sizeable map-reading error that took them on an unscheduled 40-minute detour. The ensuing three-hour drive south to Toronto was spirited, to say the least, with Bob trying to make up lost ground on his fellow competitors. After making the Toronto checkpoint with moments to spare, the crew headed out of the city once again, with conditions deteriorating to such a degree that one stage was cancelled. Only later did it emerge that this was due to the marshals involved being unable to access the checkpoint on the stage, despite having the use of a Land-Rover!

Bob's final escapade on the rally was an unplanned 'off' down a bank and into what appeared to be a frozen lake. Bizarrely, and fortuitously, rather than there being many fathoms of water beneath the ice, there was in fact a void of only a few feet, the water having drained away during a dry (but presumably still very cold) period. With assistance from a few fellow Montreal starters – who must have racked up significant time penalties and were therefore no longer in contention – Tim and Bob managed to extricate the XK and resume the rally, the valiant Jaguar showing no ill effects from the experience.

The rest of the rally passed

Upon its arrival in Canada, 660725 would assume the third registration number of its then-short life. Basking in the Ontarian sun – and with its front valance suffering from the ravages of the Canadian winter – the XK shows off its new 'Crown' embossed licence plates, as issued in Canada's Capital Province.
Bob Henderson Collection

without incident – aside from a bemusing protest (later dismissed) about an earlier potential infringement – and the XK duo were found to have been the only Montreal starters with a penalty-free run and were adjudged the winners.

Exhausted and elated after almost three days on the go with only a couple of hours of rest in Sunbury, Bob later wrote that, 'The rally had its risks… and required excessive stamina, willpower to fight sleep… mental and physical tenacity and quite a lot of mental activity as I was my own navigator most of the time, as well as being both drivers.

'I am not trying to blow my own trumpet, but it must have been rather like driving two Le Mans 24-hour races single-handed, with only a short break in between.'

Miraculously, the XK appeared to be running as strongly after the rally as it had been before, with only a few scuffs and scratches to show for it.

Expansion of Bob's business was such that he found himself working less and less at Spartan Air Services, and soon the decision was reached to concentrate full-time on the car business and maintain a consultative arrangement with SAS. Service agencies for Renault, Peugeot, Borgward and Volvo were followed by those for Aston Martin, AC and Alfa Romeo, with the associated workload growing exponentially. However, by the winter of 1958-'59, it was becoming clear that this rapid expansion was not sustainable and was starting to take its toll on Bob. This, coupled with birth of daughter Laura in October 1958 and the deteriorating health of Bob's father, meant that the decision was taken to return to the UK during the spring of the following year.

> 'I am not trying to blow my own trumpet, but it must have been rather like driving two Le Mans 24-hour races single-handed'

Conquering ice and snow • 1956-1959

Chapter Four
In and out of hibernation 1959-2004

On 24 April 1959, Prue, Laird and Laura boarded an aeroplane to return to the UK, with Bob following a week or so later having resolved a few last-minute business matters. Several factors influenced their decision to head home, not least that Bob's father was gravely ill and a return would enable him to spend valuable time with his young grandchildren.

In addition, Bob had concerns about the children being raised within the confines of the North American educational system, and he had also been offered a potentially lucrative deal by Eric Liebman to manufacture and distribute Minnow Fish carburettors in Europe.

The trusty XK 120 returned in May 1959 – complete with a boot full of sample Fish carburettors – assuming once again its UK registration number MOW 523. By this time, the original twin 1¾in SU carburettor set-up had been replaced by a single 1.55in Fish, which, intriguingly, involved blanking off one of the SU ports. Logic suggested that this would not work, although practice proved otherwise. Not only did the engine function more smoothly and with better throttle response than before, but it also proved more economical and negated the need for a choke mechanism. For some time, MOW served as a useful Fish demonstrator car and everyday means of transport, including the odd trip from the family home in Surrey up to the Hendersons' Scottish holiday retreat.

As the Minnow Fish agency took off, the poor XK suffered from a degree of mechanical and cosmetic neglect, although Bob's fertile mind ensured that it was far from forgotten about. He had long had ideas of carrying out an overdrive conversion, principally to improve fuel consumption and reduce revs on the long runs between Surrey

After some 30 years in hibernation, MOW's restoration commenced in earnest in 2000. Here it is shown on Bob's dolly trailer for transportation to local paint sprayer Archie John McVicar of Achnamara, based only seven miles or so from Bob's home in Lochgilphead.
Bob Henderson Collection

In and out of hibernation • 1959-2004

The photographs on this and the preceding page clearly show off the aluminium bonnet, door skins and boot – in contrast to the steel of the remainder of the XK's bodywork.
Bob Henderson Collection

In view of the amount of time that MOW had spent in Canada and Scotland, its bodywork remained in remarkably good condition. The sills and the seam between the rear wing and rear tonneau section are always notorious rust traps on XKs, but MOW showed little sign of significant corrosion in either area, which was testament to Bob's fastidious maintenance.
Bob Henderson Collection

In and out of hibernation • 1959-2004

'A shorter and balanced propshaft was procured – from Jack Brabham's garage in Chessington, no less – although pressures of work meant that the project was never completed'

and Scotland. Having acquired – for the nominal sum of £2 – a Jaguar MkVII with a suitable donor gearbox, Bob set about accommodating the extra length of the overdrive unit within the XK 120 chassis some time in either 1963 or 1964.

Initially, it was hoped that the conversion would simply involve changing the rear gearbox mount and sourcing a shorter propshaft, but on further inspection it was revealed that the top corner of the chassis crossmember (into which the rear gearbox mounting fitted) would require modification as well. A shorter and balanced propshaft was

The Minnow Fish carburettor

Originally designed by American inventor John Robert Fish in the 1930s, the principal aims of the Minnow Fish carburettor were to minimise fuel wastage and increase power efficiency via a superior atomisation, and hence combustion, process. With a strong background in studying pressure differentials – having assisted with the development of the Iron Lung – Fish was well qualified to understand the theory behind efficient carburettor design.

He immediately identified that conventional float chambers allowed fuel to move around excessively under acceleration, braking and cornering, and that small carburettors operated more efficiently at lower revs but became progressively less so as revs were increased. In order to compensate for this transition, larger (or multiple) carburettors would be required, which would then adversely affect fuel consumption and flexibility.

Fish therefore designed a carburettor with a single progressive metering groove that eliminated the need for conventional main and corrector jets, and which was immediately self-adjusting to accommodate any changes in climate or altitude.

Furthermore, in direct contrast to conventional units that had a single fuel discharge point, Fish carburettors in some cases had up to 10 separate feeds, which permitted a far superior atomisation process. With fuel vapour being much more combustible than the liquid itself, this improved combustion and enabled more power to be produced for a given amount of fuel than with conventional carburettors.

Popularised in the early days by NASCAR star – and later Daytona 500 winner – Glenn 'Fireball' Roberts, Fish carburettors came to be seen as a threat to the established manufacturers, who took every available opportunity to discredit the emerging technology. Although never proven, rumours of skulduggery on their part abounded, with Roberts's car suffering from more than its fair share of curious retirements…

By the mid-1950s, the now Florida-domiciled Fish had attracted financial backing from Canadian Eric Liebman, who in turn was awarded the rights to produce Fish carburettors for the Northern States, Canada and the rest of the world. Through his Ottawa-based European Car Specialists concern, Bob had met Liebman in 1956 and soon afterwards was granted a dealership. Upon his return to the UK in 1959, Bob identified a sizeable potential market for smaller Fish variants – largely based around the burgeoning sales of the new Mini – which led to Liebman granting him the rights for the rest of the world, and his subsequent patenting and manufacture of the Minnow Fish range of carburettors.

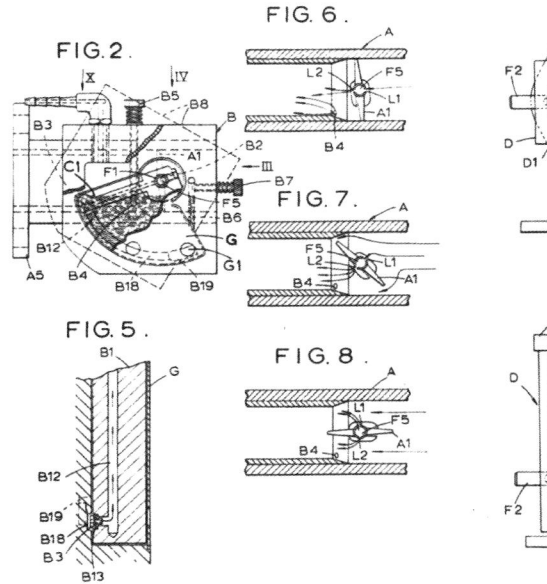
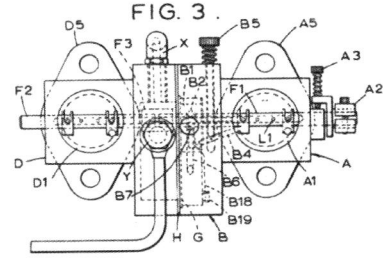
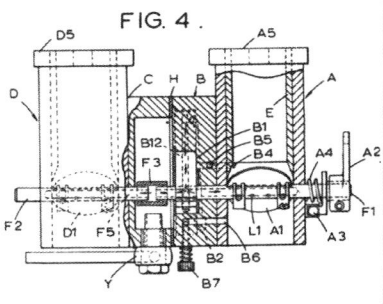

A major benefit of the Minnow Fish carburettor was dispensing with conventional jets, which rendered it self-adjusting given changes in climate or altitude. Pictured is a twin-choke version, which Bob Henderson patented.
Bob Henderson Collection

procured – from Jack Brabham's garage in Chessington, no less – although pressures of work meant that sadly the project was never completed.

Following Bob's permanent move up to Scotland in 1970, MOW was transported to his new home in Lochgilphead, on the picturesque shores of Loch Gilp in Argyll and Bute. 'The XK120… was rather abandoned in a damp garage. It, over the ensuing years, became covered in all sorts of rubbish, including a box of rotting, sprouting potatoes! Pressure of business (that's my only excuse) meant that the car was all but forgotten about for the next 30 years.'

In 2000, his conscience having been pricked by the looming 50th anniversary of his ownership, Bob commenced MOW's long-overdue restoration. Although looking rather sorry for itself, it was at least complete, and intriguingly the Michelin X tyres were still inflated due to the use of 'Air Stop' Butyl (as opposed to conventional rubber) inner tubes all those years ago!

The car was totally stripped, with all the major components overhauled and any perishable items – such as bushes, shackles and ball joints – all either refurbished or replaced as necessary. Many layers of paint were removed from the body, which revealed the myriad minor repairs that had taken place over the years.

Of particular note was the area forward of the passenger door, which showed evidence of thousands of tiny hammer marks. As Bob points out, this was not unlike a hammered pewter finish, and formed part of a repair during the car's time in Malaya, most likely as a result of an unscheduled 'off' following a CT ambush.

With MOW being an early series XK 120 – and hence fitted with the scarce but leak-prone studless cam covers – the decision was taken to remove the original engine and to replace it with the unit from the MkVII. This was duly rebuilt with new piston rings and main bearing caps, and had the added benefit of being a later unit with the all-important two additional cam cover studs, and far less susceptible to oil leaks.

With commendable forethought, Bob had retained the section of the chassis crossmember that had been removed for the abortive overdrive conversion, and this was welded back in place together with the original-style rear gearbox mount. This enabled the non-overdrive Moss

A newly repainted MOW, returned to its original silver for the first time in almost 50 years, awaiting its replacement engine. The XK's original headlight pods were retained in the restoration, albeit no longer containing spare ammunition as they had in Malaya!
Bob Henderson Collection

gearbox to be refitted once it had been mated to the rebuilt MkVII engine, which was dimensionally identical to the unit it replaced.

For the all-important respray, Bob entrusted the car to local man Archie John McVicar of Achnamara, a small village only seven or so miles from Lochgilphead. Archie had a reputation as the finest car restorer and paint sprayer in the area, and for fastidious attention to detail – something that was borne out by MOW being in his care for almost two years! After much deliberation, it was decided to return the Jaguar to its original silver colour, a choice vindicated in today's classic-car climate in which original colour schemes are considered infinitely preferable to 'non-period' hues.

MOW 523 returned to Lochgilphead in 2002 and, while this unfortunately meant that the goal of the car being completed in time for its 50th anniversary was not met, it did allow Bob to progress with the remainder of the restoration. A full retrim was undertaken, once again with the correct blue leather, carpet and vinyl as originally fitted – the majority of which Bob completed himself. The car was rewired using a replacement wiring loom, and new plywood floorboards were fabricated to replace those

A somewhat begrimed Bob, together with the XK's replacement engine, which had been removed from a MkVII saloon and purchased for the princely sum of £2. Critically, the later engine boasted three additional studs to the front of each cam cover, which offered an effective solution to the cam box oil leaks that plagued the earlier 'studless' engines.
Bob Henderson Collection

'It was decided to return the car to its original silver, a choice vindicated in today's classic-car climate in which original colour schemes are considered infinitely preferable to non-period hues'

that had rotted away during the car's lengthy hibernation. Interestingly, the original instruments and switchgear, including the cigarette lighter that had proved so useful in powering the demister unit in Canada, were all found to be in perfect working order.

Certain mechanical concessions to modernity were made. An electric fan was fitted in place of the original water pump-driven cast-alloy item, and a modern Facet fuel pump employed in place of the original SU unit. The slightly wider wheels of the MkVII were fitted and were found to improve rear-end stability without the need to increase tyre pressures (and hence encounter a deterioration in ride quality).

Finally, the installation of the single Minnow Fish carburettor was modified so that it was mounted centrally, as opposed to offset as before.

Once completed, the car looked better than it ever had done, primarily as a result of the advancement in the quality of automotive paints over the ensuing five decades. However, always the innovator, Bob identified certain areas in which he thought the car could still be improved, which will be covered in detail in the next two chapters.

The newly completed MOW, complete with its period-correct Universal Laminations hardtop. The Scintilla indicators fitted during the car's time in Indonesia have yet to be refitted at this stage.
Bob Henderson Collection

In and out of hibernation • 1959-2004

Chapter Five
Stopping power

While the XK 120 offered prodigious performance – especially in the context of the comparatively pedestrian early post-war era – it did not take long for complaints to emerge that its drum brakes were susceptible to fade after prolonged and spirited motoring. It was clear that, even though the twin-cam XK engine represented cutting-edge technology at the time, the development of brakes had not kept pace with this.

Indeed, a contemporary technical analysis in *Automobile Engineer* magazine commented that: 'In a car of this type, braking presents a particularly difficult problem and it will be noted that air scoops are fitted to the backplates of the front brake drums to assist with cooling.'

Although the earliest recorded fitment of disc brakes went back as far as the turn of the century, they were generally slow to catch on in the automotive sector. Their use on aircraft had been relatively commonplace since the 1930s, although the demands in this application – in which they would only be required perhaps once every few hours, as opposed to every few seconds – were very different.

Disc brakes were not offered as an option on Jaguar XKs until the XK 150 in 1960, and the fact that a car as technically advanced as the Mercedes-Benz 300SLR developed a bizarre air brake to supplement its existing drum braking system for Le Mans in 1955 says much of the automotive industry's reluctance to embrace the emerging technology. Significantly, Jaguar had pioneered disc brakes two years earlier and had become the first manufacturer to win the endurance classic using the technology courtesy of its Dunlop disc-equipped C-type.

In MOW's early competition outings, the brakes were found

After years of dissatisfaction with the XK's drum brakes, Bob set about designing his own disc brake system. The images opposite and overleaf show the replacement milled brake backplate, which picked up on the four $7/16$in UNF mounting holes of the original front suspension upright.
Bob Henderson Collection

Stopping power

Another view of the backplate. The shouldered 12-point bolts to the left were used to secure the brake caliper to the backplate.
Bob Henderson Collection

'A near-miss with a BMW on a local Argyll road in the late 2000s led to Bob veering onto the wrong side of the road to avoid hitting the car in question, and would precipitate a significant change in MOW's braking system'

to be adequate, although Bob identified that they were prone to fade on long descents – particularly on one celebrated occasion descending Fraser's Hill while trying to evade CT bullets! Having experimented with a variety of linings in place of the original Mintex M.15 material, Bob eventually settled on a Duron commercial lining with which he persisted for many years, although this did require noticeably higher pedal pressure to be applied in order for it to work effectively.

A near-miss with a BMW on a local Argyll road in the late 2000s led to Bob veering onto the wrong side of the road to avoid hitting the car in question, and would precipitate a significant change in MOW's braking system. Initial research indicated that

The newly designed backplate, this time with the original-style four-stud hub mounted onto the stub axle, awaiting the fitment of the brake disc and caliper.
Bob Henderson Collection

for a 'period' XK 150 disc brake system to be fitted, MOW would have to be changed from its original steel wheels to their wire counterparts in order to accommodate the bulky calipers. Furthermore, the original early-type ENV back axle only had provision for bolt-on hubs, so this would have to be changed to a later Salisbury version as well – at considerable cost. With his customary ability to think laterally, Bob set about devising his own disc-braking system that would enable the original steel wheels to be retained.

Having scoured the parts manuals of braking component suppliers such as TRW and Quinton Hazell, Bob decided on a suitable oversize disc that could then be machined down in both diameter and thickness to provide the necessary clearances and offset inside the wheel. Proprietary four-pot calipers were sourced of a sufficient size to enable them to be machined down so as to not foul on the internal rivets of the wheel, while the calipers would be mounted on a new machined offset mounting plate that would be fitted to the stub axle, thereby in effect replacing the original brake backplate.

Modifications also took place to the hydraulic system because there was a mismatch between the original-fitment 1/4in brake pipes on the car and the more modern components intended for use in conjunction with pipes of only 3/16in bore. To compensate for this, Bob fitted a calibrated restrictor at the junction of the original-size brake hose and the caliper bridge pipe. Consideration was briefly given to a dual-circuit system in which the front-to-rear bias could be easily adjusted via a brake balance bar, but this was eventually ruled out on the grounds of complexity and it being an unnecessary deviation from the original system.

After minor troubleshooting and calibration, the conversion was viewed as an unqualified success, with the rear wheels found to lock up just before the fronts, as intended. At the car's first MoT after the conversion, it was discovered that the new system afforded two and a half times the braking power of the drum set-up for the same level of pedal pressure.

As a very contented Bob was moved to comment afterwards: 'On the road, the braking at all speeds is vastly improved and always evenly balanced – compared to the variable drums – even in the wet and icy conditions that you find in the West Highlands.'

'At the car's first MoT after the conversion, it was discovered that the new system afforded two and a half times the braking power of the drum set-up for the same level of pedal pressure'

The completed front braking assembly, with disc and proprietary four-pot caliper fitted. The latter items were machined down slightly in order to fit within the confines of the XK's original-equipment steel disc wheels, thereby preserving the original aesthetics of the car.
Bob Henderson Collection

Chapter Six

Turbocharging an XK 120!

The standard specification, 8:1 compression ratio, 3.4-litre XK engine had, on its introduction, been rated at 160bhp at 5,000rpm, with a corresponding maximum torque figure of 195lb ft at only 2,500rpm. Performance figures that were recorded in period vary considerably, partly due to variations in specifications in individual cars and partly due to the comparatively crude timing and measuring equipment that was then available. However, the 1948 Motor Show car was tested by *The Motor* in November 1949. Chassis 660001, which had been driven by Prince Bira in the fabled Silverstone Production Car race earlier that year, established a maximum speed of 124.6mph, with a 0-60mph time of exactly 10 seconds.

Some 60 or so years later, Bob Henderson – having pioneered early turbocharging of production cars as diverse as an 850cc Steyr-Puch and 5.3-litre Pontiac Firebird back in the 1970s – decided to consider the possibility of carrying out the same procedure on MOW.

The underlying aim of a turbo is to increase the efficiency and power output of any given engine by forcing compressed air, via an exhaust gas-driven turbine, into the combustion chamber. A proportionate increase in the amount of fuel introduced at the same time results in a bigger 'burn', which in turn leads to more power being produced per engine cycle.

While the volumetric efficiency – the ratio of air volume actually drawn into the cylinder relative to that cylinder's swept volume – of a normally aspirated car tends to be in the range of 70-80 percent, with turbocharged engines it is not uncommon to see a corresponding figure in excess of 100 percent.

Bob had championed turbocharging for many years

The mocked-up installation of the Garrett-type Roto-Master turbocharger, with the exhaust manifold and exhaust pipe affixed behind. The small bore right-angled fitting to the top of the unit is the oil feed, vital to the safe and efficient operation of any turbocharger.
Bob Henderson Collection

The inlet side of the engine, with the Minnow Fish carburettor in the foreground and the pressure box on top. The latter was tailored to the bonnet contours. The blow-off valve is also visible, just below and to the rear of the pressure box.
Bob Henderson Collection

as being a highly effective way of obtaining a significant power increase for only a relatively modest increase in weight. With remarkable prescience, some 45 years ago he wrote that: 'The only long-term saviour [of the motor car] will be the blown engine, which can double or treble the power output for only a 10-20 percent increase in weight. Since the cost and complexity could be less than the much-vaunted fuel-injection systems – which offer only marginally improved efficiency – this is obviously the way to go.'

On first inspection, it was clear that any turbocharging system for MOW would present certain ergonomic and installation problems due to the proximity of the bodywork and other under-bonnet components. The routing of the hot exhaust was to prove problematic, as was the proximity of the single Minnow Fish carburettor to the bonnet, which left virtually no 'headroom' above it.

Assisted by his long-time right-hand man Iver Ferguson, Bob fabricated his own 3in-bore exhaust system, which was finished off with a length of copper pipe for added sound effects! A contoured collector box (with integral boost pop-off valve) was also fabricated to avoid it fouling the bonnet and to allow for engine movement under load, with the main feed pipe from the turbo passing underneath the car. The presence of the shallower sump of the MkVII engine was a great help in this respect – the much larger-capacity sump of the original engine would have presented serious ground-clearance issues. In addition, passing the feed pipe underneath the car meant that it was, in effect, operating as a crude intercooler. As with any turbocharged engine, the cooler the intake air can be kept, the greater the volumetric efficiency.

Provision was made for additional crankcase breathing because turbo engines not surprisingly tend to experience higher crankcase pressures than their normally aspirated counterparts. Similarly, oil feeds to and from the turbo were both accommodated, because the incredible speeds with which turbos operate mean that efficient lubrication is critical. Inevitably, any oil passing around

Turbocharging an XK 120

The fabricated flanges for the modified XK exhaust manifold, in the process of being milled 'in house' at Bob's workshops in Lochgilphead.
Bob Henderson Collection

The Argyll Turbo GT

Reviving the name of arguably Scotland's most illustrious motor manufacturer, the Argyll Turbo GT was the brainchild of Bob Henderson and was aimed squarely – if, with hindsight, somewhat optimistically – at breaking into the burgeoning 1970s supercar market.

Bravely, Bob took the decision to manufacture (or to modify, from proprietary components) the majority of the car in-house. By making use of the existing facilities at his Lochgilphead workshop, it was hoped that the Argyll would be both relatively cost-effective to manufacture and unencumbered by complex supply chains or production delays.

It featured a complex steel spaceframe chassis, to which a heavy-gauge fibreglass body was bonded for additional strength, and separate subframes were employed front and rear for ease of assembly and maintenance. Although the 1976 prototype had a turbocharged 3.5-litre Rover V8, various other power options were available, including the 2.7-litre PRV (Peugeot-Renault-Volvo) 'Douvrin' V6, which came in either normally aspirated or turbocharged form. Transmission was a choice of a production-based Renault or race-derived ZF transaxle, while the suspension featured conventional twin wishbones with coil springs and telescopic damper units.

With adjustable seats, steering column and pedal box, and the ingenious roof-recessed rear-view mirror, the interior was redolent of rear-engined sports-racers such as the Ford GT40, although the finest Scottish leather seats and Wilton carpets offered a far superior standard of finish.

The exterior, however, divided opinion: to some it was futuristic and purposeful; to others it was gawky and an acquired taste. At almost 10ft, it was noticeably long in the wheelbase – the corresponding dimension on a Ferrari 308 was 7ft 8in.

Performance was broadly in line with its contemporaries, with the normally aspirated 2.7-litre version offering a maximum speed of around 140mph, while the turbocharged 3.5-litre V8 offered an additional 20mph and a 0-60mph time of under six seconds.

Initial development work was carried out both on the road and on the forest stages by former Scottish Rally Champion Andrew Smith, and the prototype was reviewed favourably by Gordon Bruce in *Motor* in September 1976.

Bruce noted that: 'After a mere mile… my inhibitions had gone and I was enjoying what can only be described as a unique motoring experience… After a couple of miles I felt at one with the chassis, and positively excited by the engine. However, by far the most impressive quality is the ride… The car coped happily with everything from high-speed ridges to town pot-holes, never bottoming and never throwing its occupants around.'

After seven long years in development, the Argyll was unveiled at Inveraray Castle in October 1983, and made its first public appearance a month later at the Scottish Motor Show in Glasgow. Sadly, its long gestation period – combined with limited funding, the ongoing effects

The distinctive Argyll GT boasted a long wheelbase to improve ride quality, but suffered from the Oil Crisis and stiff competition from the likes of the Porsche 911.
Argyll/Bob Henderson Collection

> 'Bob also carried out performance tests, which provided some startling results. From 0-100mph, the average reading was a barely believable 13.8 seconds'

of the 1970s Oil Crisis and the comparatively sporadic nature of production – meant that the project struggled to generate any meaningful momentum.

Its bespoke nature was not in doubt, but some of the component choices were – to put it mildly – curious. At a rumoured cost of between £25,000-30,000 (at a time when a Porsche 911 was roughly £21,000), it's not surprising that there were dissenting voices concerning the use of Morris Marina door handles, Datsun Cherry rear lights, a Volvo dashboard and a Triumph Dolomite steering wheel.

Initially, it was hoped that one car would be produced per month in Lochgilphead, with production rising to a possible 30 cars per year. Bob was encouraged to shift production to a dedicated factory in Glasgow but – with commendable loyalty to his small, local workforce – he opted to stay in Lochgilphead.

He remains coy as to the extent of final production, remarking only that it was 'dozens rather than hundreds', and no more than a handful are thought to remain in circulation. Fittingly, one example remains on permanent display in the Grampian Transport Museum near Aberdeen, an intriguing reminder of one of the great 'might have beens' of small-scale British motor manufacturing.

a turbo habitually operating at several hundred degrees centigrade heats up far more than in a normally aspirated engine, so for this reason an oil cooler was also fitted to keep temperatures within acceptable limits.

Finally, a high-pressure fuel pump was fitted to accommodate the additional fuelling demands of the newly turbocharged engine. Here, fuel from the pump feeds into a swirl pot, which ensures that a good 'head' of fuel is maintained, and that the fuel remains unaerated. In effect, the swirl pot operates on a very similar principle to an oil tank in a dry-sump lubrication system. As boost is applied to the turbo, the system automatically compensates by increasing the fuel pressure, thus ensuring that the carburettor is always supplied with sufficient fuel.

Following extensive dynamometer testing, the new installation was found to produce an impressive 298bhp at 7½psi boost, and some 321bhp at 12psi. An early road test showed that both torque and flexibility – characteristics that the original unit already possessed in abundance – were further enhanced, with the car pulling strongly from just 2,000rpm and producing maximum boost between 3-3,500rpm.

Bob also carried out performance tests, which provided some startling results. From

0-100mph, the average reading was a barely believable 13.8 seconds, in comparison to 28.3 seconds for the standard car. Despite the XK 120 weighing an additional 3cwt, this compared favourably with the 16 seconds recorded for a standard E-type. In mitigation, the XK tests were carried out with a lower final-drive ratio fitted (thought to be costing roughly 4mph per 1,000rpm in top gear, but with a corresponding improvement in acceleration) and the Universal Laminations hardtop in place, but nevertheless the results were indisputable.

However, despite the significant performance gains, Bob offered some typically honest thoughts on the conversion: 'Would I recommend it? Even allowing for the disc brake conversion, the simple answer is no, because it changes the whole character of the car such that one feels almost lost to another age and realm. It is just no longer an XK 120.'

Another not-insignificant consideration was that, while the performance had moved forward dramatically, this was of only limited use given that much of the rest of the car remained in its original specification. Although the disc brake conversion meant that there was at least an efficient means of slowing down,

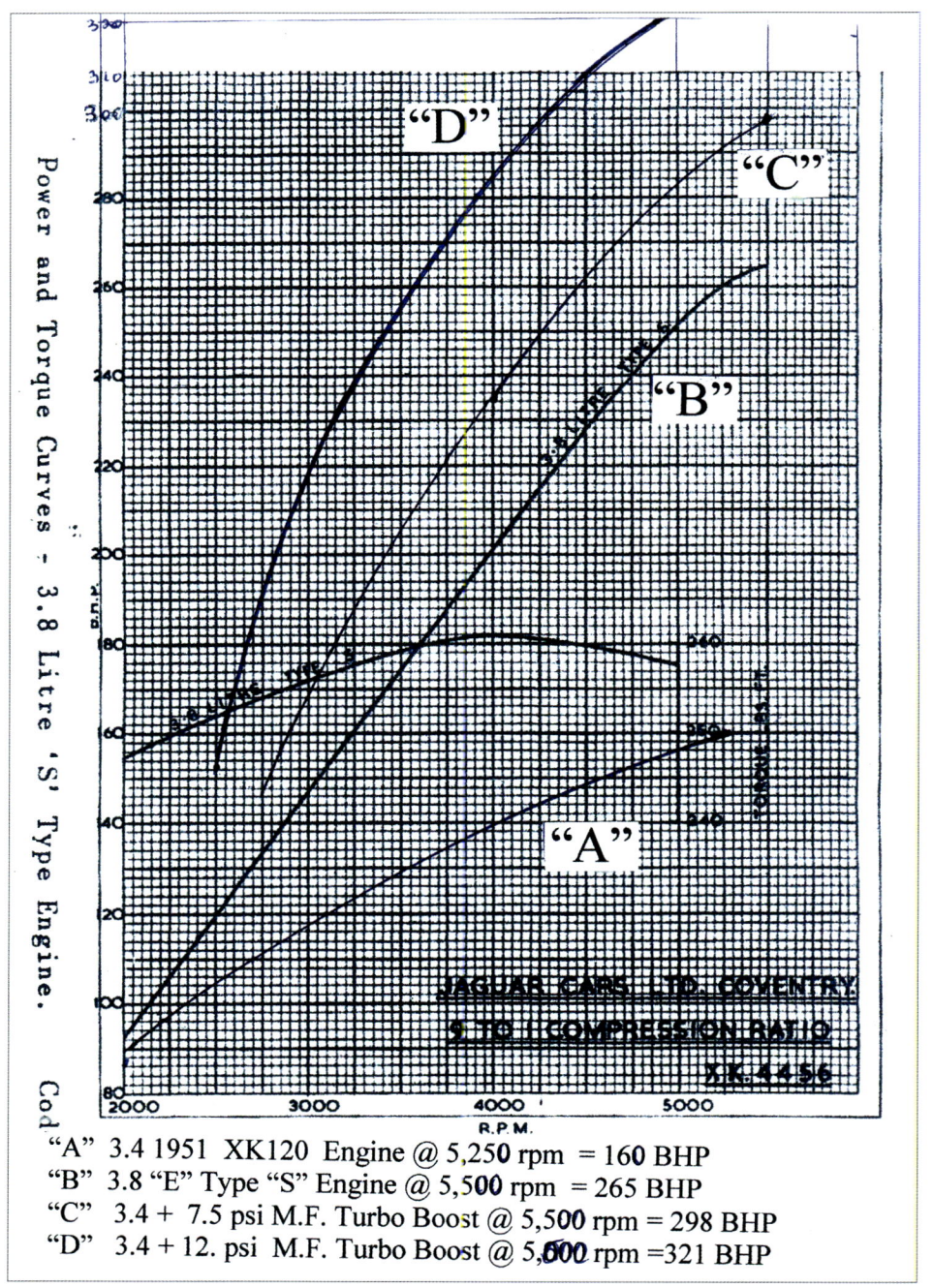

A graph showing the relative power curves of the standard 3.4-litre XK engine (A), 3.8-litre 'straight port' E-type engine, (B) and the modified 'Minnow Fish' 3.4-litre versions with 7.5psi and 12psi turbo boost respectively (C and D). Bob Henderson Collection

> 'While a fascinating exercise, Bob was firmly of the opinion that the ultimate XK should remain normally aspirated'

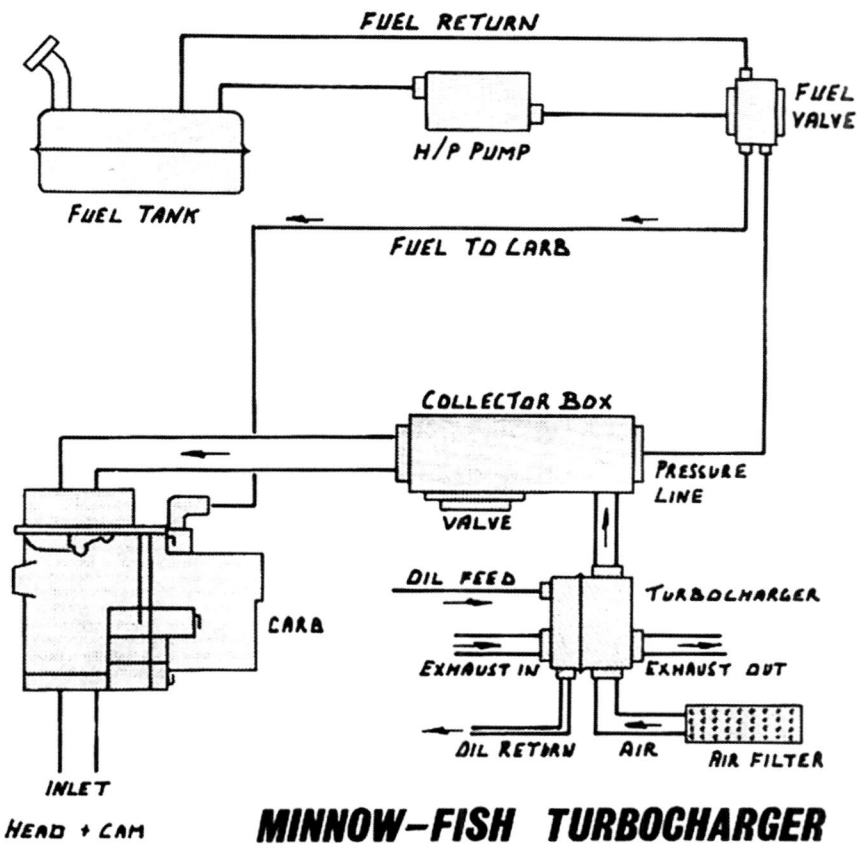

Fig. 24 – Minnow-Fish automatically adjustable fuel feed system.

A schematic diagram showing the flow directions and relative positions of the various critical components in the Minnow Fish turbocharger installation, as fitted to MOW.
Bob Henderson Collection

other areas such as handling, ride and traction had not been addressed, and so these now became the limiting factors.

While a fascinating technical exercise, and something that admirably showcased the talents of his tuning concern, Bob was firmly of the opinion that the ultimate XK should remain normally aspirated. That this could be done with a 'period correct' 3.4-litre C- or D-type engine, of possibly 250-260bhp, or a modern enlarged-capacity unit of rather greater power, as produced by companies such as Rob Beere Racing or Eagle, speaks volumes for the longevity and near-infinite variety of options within the XK or XK-derived engine range.

Chapter Seven
Postscript

Although the lengthy rebuild of MOW was completed in 2004, for some time it was tested only on local roads in Argyll – making use of Bob's trade plates – and did not actually obtain an MoT until 2007. However, after a further six years' enjoyment, and 62 years' ownership in total, Bob took the brave but difficult decision that it was time for the car to be enjoyed by someone else. At this stage, the turbocharger was removed from the car, but the Minnow Fish carburettor and disc brake conversion were left in place.

Having placed an ad in the *XK Gazette* in August 2013, the car was sold to an overseas enthusiast in February 2015. Fittingly, it was accompanied by the original engine block, 'studless' cylinder head, alloy sump, original drum brake components, and unusual but very period-correct Universal Laminations hardtop. Remarkably, at this point the car had covered a mere 23,000 miles in its eventful 64-year life.

It had long been the new owner's ambition to compete in classic road rallies such as the Mille Miglia retrospective – a gruelling and prestigious event for which an XK 120 is ideally suited. However, in order for MOW to be eligible for the Italian classic, several modifications would be required to return the car to its original specification and a comprehensive mechanical overhaul carried out. Both elements are covered in the final chapter overleaf.

This portrait of Bob and his second wife Fay in the newly restored MOW 523 at their house in Lochgilphead in 2004 would seem a fitting photographic conclusion. Although the restoration work was completed that year, the XK would not actually receive an MoT for another three years – although this did not prevent Bob from extensively road-testing the car on trade plates in the meantime.
Bob Henderson Collection

Postscript

Chapter Eight
MOW 523 in detail
Studio photography by John Colley

Soon after it passed to the current owner, the XK was entrusted to Classic Motor Cars of Bridgnorth, Shropshire, which has previously restored several significant Jaguars. These include the 'Lindner-Nöcker' Lightweight E-type, the ex-works D-type OKV 1, and 9600 HP – the famous pre-production E-type used at the Geneva launch.

The brief was succinct and sympathetic: to restore the car to original specification using the all-important factory components that accompanied the sale, yet preserve the originality and patina of a near-70-year-old car. MOW was reunited with its original cylinder head and SU carburettors, and a full engine rebuild was carried out. The rear axle was removed and rebuilt, while the non-period disc brakes were removed and replaced by the original and newly rebuilt drums.

MOW's cosmetic appearance, both inside and out, was left unchanged. The only non-standard items that appear on the Jaguar are those fitted by Bob Henderson – in many cases when the car was only a handful of years old. The attention to detail and sympathy with which the rebuild has been carried out is remarkable, the retention of the period tax discs and Bob's Mosquito Aircrew Association windscreen sticker being a particularly nice touch.

The rebuild was completed in early 2020, and it is this form in which 660725 appears in the subsequent pages.

MOW 523 as it appears today, fresh from its recent restoration. With the exception of the addition of racing roundels and the Jaguar saloon-type bonnet mascot, which was fitted to the car by Bob Henderson in the mid-1950s, 660725 now appears exactly as it did when it left the Coventry factory in 1951.

MOW 523 in detail

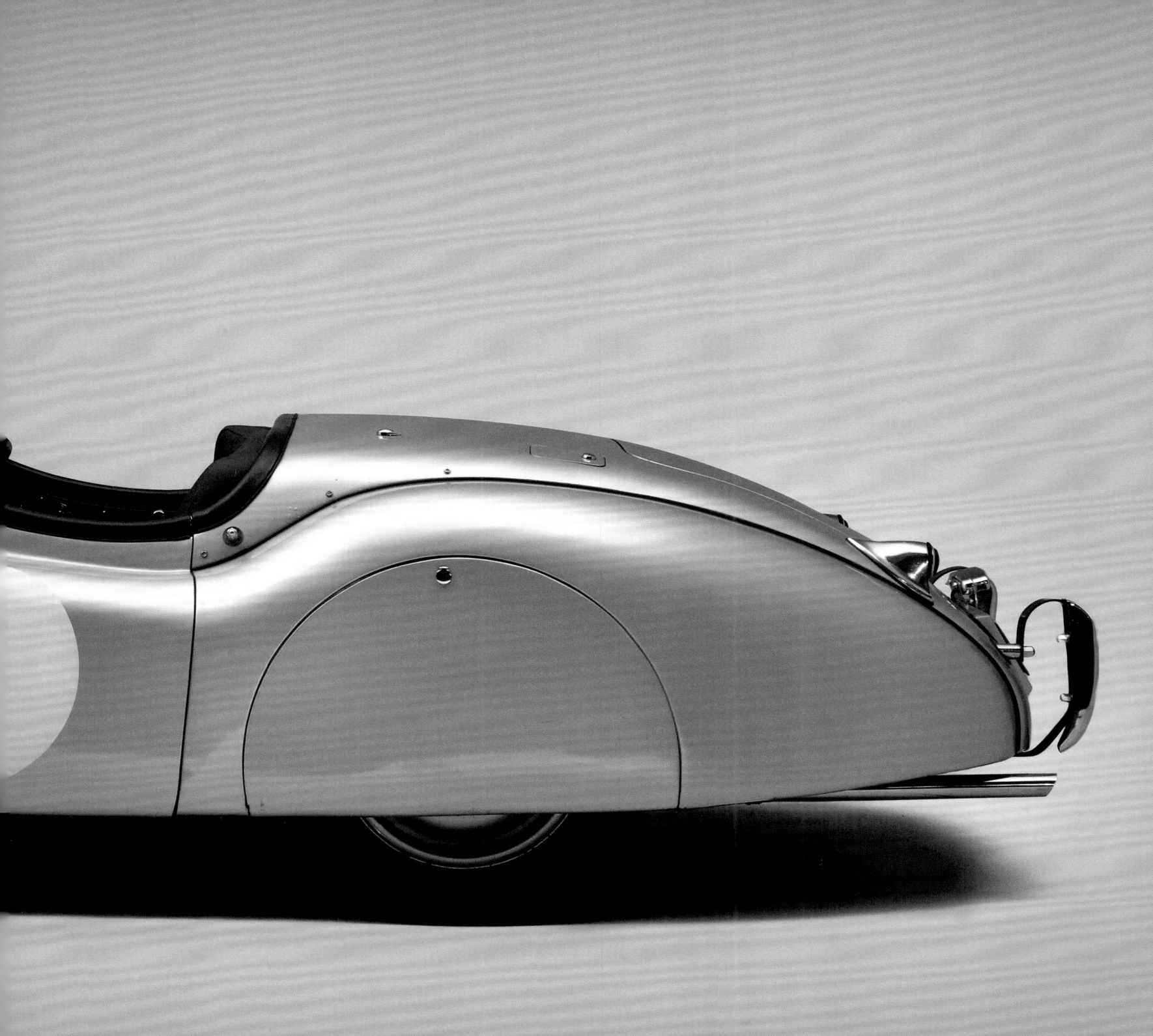

During restoration, 660725's original early-type 'studless' cylinder head was refitted to the car, as shown on the opposite page. Part of the sympathetic restoration brief that CMC received was to retain, wherever possible, period components and finishes in order to preserve the car's originality. The fitment of the original brass chassis plate, detailing chassis, engine, gearbox and body numbers, and the retention of the original patinated finish of the engine compartment, are but two examples of this.

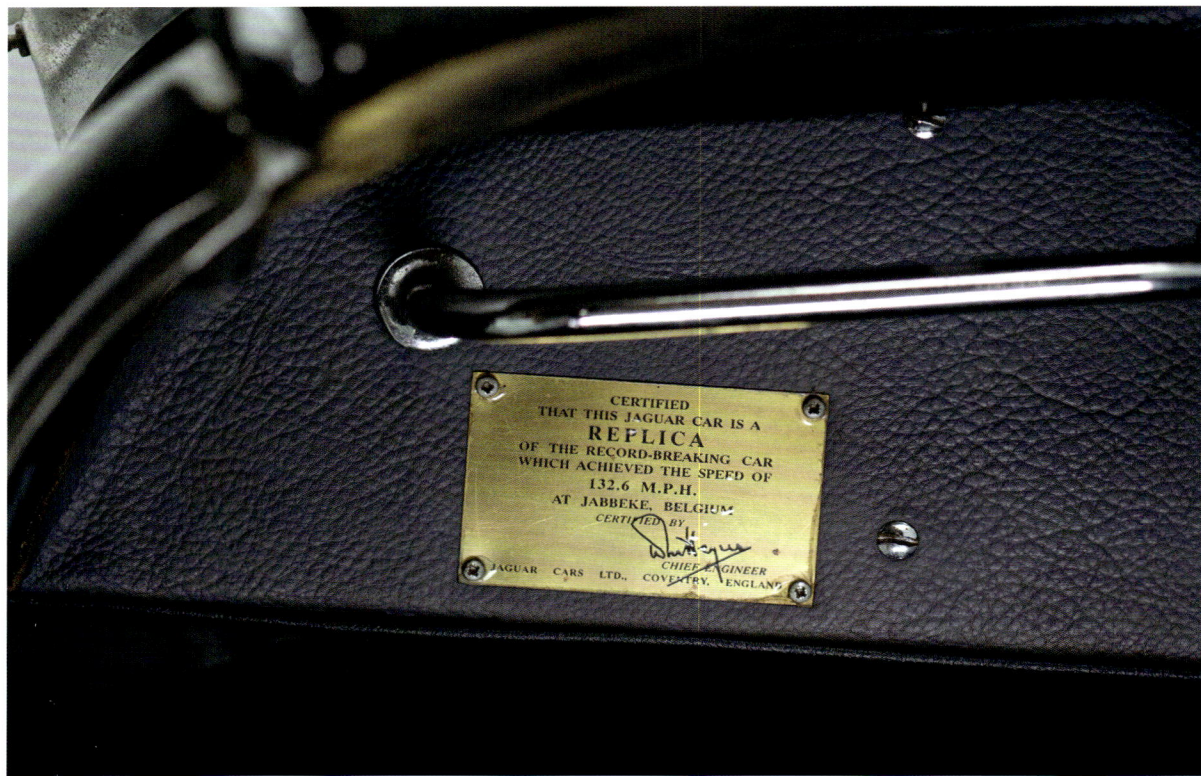

The majority of standard 8:1 compression XK 120 Roadsters prepared for the export market were fitted with a brass plaque commemorating the efforts of Jaguar test driver Ron 'Soapy' Sutton at Jabbeke in Belgium, in 1949. Sutton's maximum speed of 132.6mph in the works-prepared XK 120 HKV 500 was, at the time, the fastest speed ever recorded by a production car. Interestingly, such a plaque is fitted to 660725, even though it was originally fitted with a lower 7:1 compression engine.

MOW 523 in detail

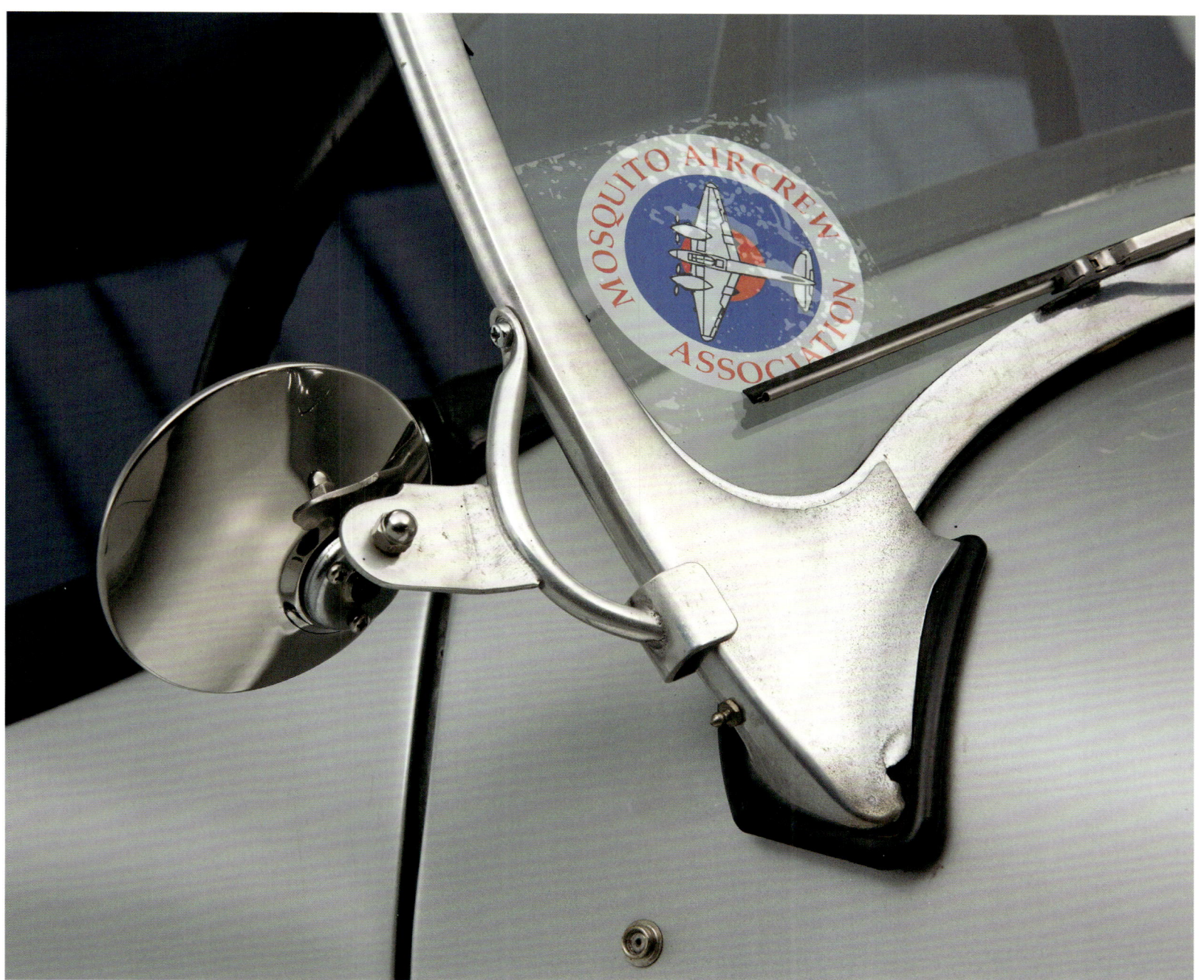

A significant proportion of surviving XK 120s have been converted from the standard steel disc-type wheels with rear spats to the more sporting wire wheel option. MOW 523 is one of only a handful of such cars to have never succumbed to the latter and, in the context of this particular chassis, incorrect modification. The timeless elegance of the car's lines is shown to great effect from this three-quarter rear angle.

MOW 523 in detail

In common with several other Jaguar series – perhaps most noticeably the E-type – the early XK 120s remain by far the most pure and aesthetically pleasing examples of their particular family. In contrast, the later XK 140s and XK 150s – while arguably providing a superior driving experience – were characterised by heavier, less subtle features such as thicker bumpers and enlarged rear lights, which to some degree compromised their respective appearances.

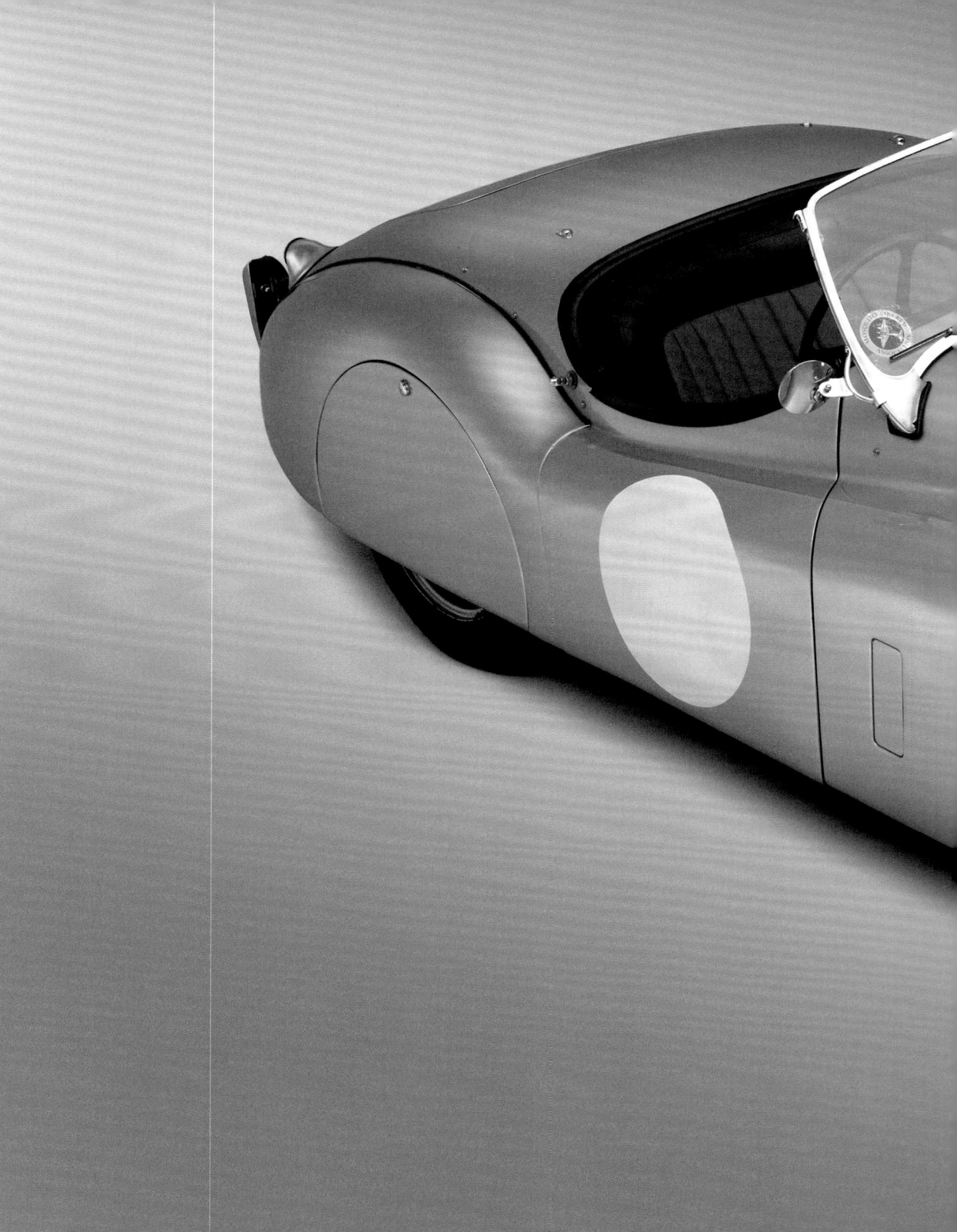

Early examples of the XK 120 OTS, such as 660725, were fitted with separate chrome sidelight pods that were bolted onto both front wings. Conversely, later OTS cars – from October 1952 onwards – were fitted with welded-in mild steel

Porter Profiles – Jaguar XK 120 • Chassis 660725

Although originally fitted with Dunlop 6.00-16 RS5 crossply tyres, many XKs are now fitted with modern radial replacements such as those available from Vredestein – as currently fitted to 660725. These combine the aesthetic appearance of the original tyre with superior roadholding and increased predictability in adverse weather conditions – not something for which the RS5 was ever renowned!

Index

Appleyard, Ian 6
Argyll GT 64
Aston Martin (company) 42
    DB3S 8
    DB4 6
Brabham, Jack 47, 49
Britannia Bay Ice Races 39, 40
Buegen Bik, Tony van 23, 28
Canadian International Winter Rally 40, 41
Choon, Chan Lye 8, 11, 12
Earls Court 6
Fish, John Robert 48
Grand Prix
    Johore 8, 23
    Macau 8
Hadley, Bert 6
Hash House 17, 18
Henderson, Bob 8, 11, 12, 13, 15, 17, 18, 19, 21, 22, 23, 24, 26, 28, 31, 32, 34, 36, 39, 40, 41, 42, 44, 47, 48, 49, 51, 52, 54, 57, 59, 60, 62, 63, 64, 65, 66, 67, 68, 70
Hoi, Ah 11, 13, 21, 22

Jaguar (company) 6, 7, 8, 11, 15, 21, 36, 39, 54, 78, 86
    C-type 6, 54
    D-type 6, 15, 67, 70
    E-type 6, 7, 66, 70, 86
    XK 120 6, 7, 8, 11, 19, 23, 24, 26, 31, 40, 44, 47, 49, 54, 60, 66, 68, 78, 83, 86, 88
    XK 140 6, 86
    XK 150 6, 7, 54, 59, 86
Johnson, Leslie 6
Kwan, Ah 11, 13, 21, 22
Lapworth, Prue 28, 34, 36, 39, 41, 44
Le Mans 6, 7, 54
    24 Hours 42
Liebman, Eric 44, 48
Lyons, Sir William 6
McRobert, Stanley 40
McVicar, Archie John 44, 51
Mille Miglia 6, 68
Minnow Fish 44, 48, 52, 62, 66, 67, 68
Mosquito, de Havilland 28, 31, 32, 33, 34, 36, 41, 70
Moss, Sir Stirling 6

Nock, Peter 31, 34
Plottier, Tim 41
Pope, Freddie 23, 24, 26
Prince Bira 60
Roberts, Glenn 'Fireball' 48
Short, Robert (Bob) 28, 31, 34
Silverstone 6
Spartan Air Services 34, 36, 42
Sutton, Ron 'Soapy' 78
Tourist Trophy 6
Walker, Peter 6

Acknowledgements

It is something of a cliché that those involved in any non-fiction book are manifold: many inspire, some are involved in the production process, while a handful are responsible – critically – for the generation of the subject matter in the first place. As someone who, from his schooldays, was regularly made aware of the importance of first-hand evidence, as opposed to relying on secondary sources, it has been a pleasure – and a huge luxury – to have the original, long-term owner of this remarkable car, Bob Henderson, at the end of a telephone throughout the production of this book.

It is a sad fact of life that most of those associated with the Jaguar XK's early successes – Sir William Lyons, Bill Heynes, Sir Stirling Moss, Norman Dewis, Ian Appleyard and Ron 'Soapy' Sutton, to name but a few – are no longer with us, which makes Bob's contribution even more valuable. His patience, good humour and, above all, remarkable recall are appreciated beyond measure, and from a personal perspective it was hugely satisfying to record his memories first-hand, almost 70 years after his initial acquaintance with the car. Furthermore, the day that I spent in his company, and that of his charming wife Faye, at their beautiful Lochgilphead home up on the West Coast of Scotland is one I shall cherish for many years to come.

Once again, it has been a delight to work with the fantastic team at Porter Press International. To Philip and Julie Porter, I extend my sincere thanks for their continued faith and for affording me the opportunity to research the story of another fascinating car. In Philip, I am also hugely fortunate in having arguably the world's pre-eminent XK authority on the proverbial speed dial, and his patience with my frequent technical and historical queries (and the occasional idiotic question!) is hugely appreciated.

I am also indebted to my Editor, James Page, for his guidance and innate organisational and grammatical skills, as I am to Martin Port and John Colley for their respective design and photographic prowess. It would also be remiss of me not to acknowledge the remainder of the PPI team past and present for their collective input: to Tania Brown, Louise Gibbs, Annelise Airey, Emily Peverell and Holly Beaumont, thank you all.

Finally, to the car's current custodian I offer my sincere thanks for his initial approach. In an era when an increasing number of historic cars are sadly being lost to anonymous private collections or – worse still – are being held in long-term secure storage due to their ever-increasing values, it is refreshing to learn of someone who appreciates the historic context of a car such as this, and who uses it as it was originally intended. With this in mind, I wish him many years of happy motoring and enjoyment ahead.

Simon Ham
Bedford, UK
October 2020

Bibliography

An unusual CV Bob Henderson
The Chequered Past: Sports Car Racing and Rallying in Canada 1951-1991 David A Charters
Original Jaguar XK Philip Porter
Norman Dewis of Jaguar Paul Skilleter with Norman Dewis
The Jaguar Companion Kenneth Ullyett
Jaguar Sports Cars Paul Skilleter
Jaguar XK 120/ XK 140 Super Profile Philip Porter
Great Marques – Jaguar Chris Harvey
Jaguar Sports Racing & Works Competition Cars to 1953 Andrew Whyte
Jaguar Enthusiast Articles by Bob Henderson, 2012-2018